D0426691

A Quiet
Courage

Also by Elizabeth R. Skoglund
   Safety Zones
   Life on the Line
   It's OK to Be a Woman Again
   Making Bad Times Good
   The Welcoming Hearth
   Wounded Heroes
   Amma

A Quiet Courage

*Per Anger, Wallenberg's
Co-Liberator of Hungarian Jews*

ELIZABETH R. SKOGLUND

BakerBooks

A Division of Baker Book House Co
Grand Rapids, Michigan 49516

© 1997 by Elizabeth R. Skoglund

Published by Baker Books
a division of Baker Book House Company
P.O. Box 6287, Grand Rapids, MI 49516-6287

Printed in the United States of America

Library of Congress Cataloging-in-Publication Data

Skoglund, Elizabeth.
    A quiet courage : Per Anger, Wallenberg's co-liberator of Hungarian Jews / Elizabeth R. Skoglund.
       p.   cm.
    Includes bibliographical references and index.
    ISBN 0-8010-1125-6
    1. Jews—Persecutions—Hungary. 2. Wallenberg, Raoul. 3. Diplo-mats—Sweden—Biography. 4. Holocaust, Jewish (1939–1945)—Hungary. 5. World War, 1939–1945—Jews—Rescue—Hungary. 6. Hungary—Ethnic relations. 7. Anger, Per, 1913–   . 8. Ambas-sadors—Sweden—Biography. 9. Righteous Gentiles in the Holocaust. I. Title.
DS135.H9S53   1997
943.9'004924—dc20   96-32993

Scripture marked TLB is taken from *The Living Bible* © 1971. Used by permis-sion of Tyndale House Publishers, Inc., Wheaton, IL 60189. All rights reserved.

To Betty and Ragnar Skoglund, my Swedish parents, whose example taught me the value of a human life and the obligation to act positively in the face of evil.

To Beryl and Walter Danielson, whose hospitality and friendship have made a difference.

The barbarity and speed with which the Hungarian Jews were destroyed has been characterized by Winston Churchill as "probably the greatest and most horrible crime ever committed in the history of the world."

Randolph L. Braham
The Politics of Genocide

As you have done to Israel, so will it be done to you.

Obadiah 15
The Living Bible

I will bless those who bless you, and I will curse him who curses you.

Genesis 12:3
New King James Version

Contents

Ambassador Per Anger and his wife, Elena, 1995. *(Photographer: David Swerdlin. Used by permission.)*

Foreword

A mbassador Per Anger of Sweden is indelibly linked in most people's minds with the Swedish humanitarian and Holocaust hero, Raoul Wallenberg. With the invaluable assistance and support of Per Anger in Budapest in 1944, Wallenberg saved tens of thousands of children, women, and men from the forced marches and from the trains bound for the extermination camps at Auschwitz and elsewhere in Nazi-occupied Europe.

Independent of his relationship with Raoul Wallenberg, however, Per Anger has had a distinguished career as a Swedish diplomat and as an advocate for humanitarian service. He served as Swedish ambassador to both Australia and Canada, he was an advocate and activist within the Swedish Foreign Ministry for humanitarian assistance, and he has been a voice of conscience in Swedish diplomacy.

While his diplomatic career is indeed most distinguished, it is his link with Raoul Wallenberg that sets Ambassador Per Anger apart, that raises him above the many eminent Swedes who have served their country with honor and with integrity. His association with Raoul Wallenberg was a defining moment for Per, and it gave him a cause that he has continued to pursue with commitment and intelligence throughout his life. Because of that association, he will be honored around the world for generations—and for a number of important and valid reasons.

First, Per Anger was Wallenberg's key associate at the Swedish legation in Budapest in 1944. The two were about the same age, but they had somewhat different backgrounds. Wallenberg, in keeping with his family tradition, was involved in business activities in Stockholm. Anger had trained and prepared himself for diplomatic service. Although Budapest was his first assignment as a diplomat, he had been in Hungary for some time before Wallenberg arrived and was better acquainted with conditions there. Per became one of Raoul's principal collaborators in his life-saving humanitarian efforts in Hungary.

Second, a great deal of what we know about Raoul Wallenberg's efforts in Budapest in 1944 is the result of the work of Per Anger. His memoir, *With Raoul Wallenberg in Budapest,* provides essential documentation of many of the events during that tempestuous time. Without this published recollection, our knowledge of Wallenberg's incredible struggle against the Nazi terror would be considerably diminished.

Third, Per Anger was a champion within the Swedish Foreign Ministry, urging bolder and more aggressive action by the Swedish government to secure the release of Raoul Wallenberg after he was seized and imprisoned in the Soviet Union in 1945. Because Sweden was reluctant to take any action that might antagonize its huge neighbor to the east, it officially pursued a cautious and pusillanimous policy in seeking the release of Wallenberg. Within the Swedish Foreign Ministry, Ambassador Anger was a strong voice for bolder action. After his retirement from the diplomatic service, Per has continued his efforts. Following the collapse of the Soviet Union, he was in Moscow on a number of occasions, at times with members of Raoul's family, in the continuing effort to determine the truth of what really happened after Wallenberg was seized by Red Army troops in Eastern Hungary in January 1945.

Fourth, Ambassador Anger has been one of the leaders in keeping alive the memory of Raoul Wallenberg. He has been an articulate advocate for Raoul and a forceful spokesman in honoring him. We remember well many occasions when Anger paid eloquent tribute to the heroism of Raoul Wallenberg. One of his most memorable and moving tributes was given at the United States Holocaust Memorial Museum in Washington, D.C., on January 17, 1995, at the commemoration of the fiftieth anniversary of Wallenberg's disappearance.

Elizabeth R. Skoglund has done a truly remarkable service in bringing together all of the diverse strands in the life of Per Anger in this excellent biography. She has provided the background that permits us to better understand and appreciate this multifaceted and diverse man. For those of us who know him principally through his Wallenberg connection, it gives us added insight into his diplomatic career. For those who know Per from his distinguished service in the Swedish Foreign Ministry, it provides a penetrating insight into the importance of his brief six months with Raoul Wallenberg in Budapest. For all of us, it provides insight into his personality, integrity, hard work, and energetic devotion to his diplomatic career and his family.

As we reflect on the unspeakable horrors that were unleashed upon the world by the Nazi regime a half-century ago, it is important that we not only remember the atrocities and violence and murder and terror of that time, but that we also consider the sparks of humanity that glowed in the midst of that darkest of midnights. Per Anger was one of those radiant sparks of light. It is always instructive and uplifting to examine the lives of such decent men and women. This biography of Ambassador Per Anger is important in helping us to understand why some individuals have the decency, dedication, and motivation to do good against incredible odds.

Tom and Annette Lantos
Washington, D.C.—July 1996

Preface

On a warm spring evening in May 1988, I went to the Simon Wiesenthal Center in Los Angeles. My interest in the center went back several years, but I had never been there before. Entering the building by walking through a metal detector, I found my way to a stark basement room where, preserved under glass, I saw some personal effects of Holocaust victims—a doll with a cracked face, a lock of hair, now-useless eyeglasses. These set the atmosphere for an evening I will never forget.

After we were seated in an area where chairs had been set up for the occasion, an expectant hush fell over the crowd, packed tightly into the small, stuffy room. A handsome man in his early seventies with white hair, an erect bearing, and a face etched with lines of kindness and compassion came to the podium. Then with breathtaking drama and quiet dignity, Swedish ambassador Per Anger[1] told of his experiences with Raoul Wallenberg in Budapest at the end of World War II.

I had heard much of the Wallenberg-Anger account of the rescue of Jews, mainly through my reading, which had included the ambassador's own book, *With Raoul Wallenberg in Budapest*.[2] Therefore, much of the ambassador's story was not unfamiliar to me, and it supported my lifelong conviction that one person can make a difference. But never before that night had I fully realized that for evil or for good, one can literally change the fate of so many people and, in so doing, alter the course of history itself.

"As long as there is a Raoul Wallenberg," the ambassador concluded, "it gives hope. One man can do much through his endeavor for righteousness."

Living proof of his words came when a man stood up and said sadly: "I was in a small town in Poland. We didn't have a Raoul Wallenberg, but we needed one." Then a woman rushed across the room and embraced the ambassador: "Do you remember me?" she asked. "You saved me twice: once in Budapest at the end of the war, and once again during the uprising of 1956." She could not have known this was not the first time Anger had heard such a testimony.

How many people were saved twice by this remarkable man? I've wondered.

On the way home that night, I knew my life had been deeply influenced, and I needed time to absorb what I had witnessed. One man, Raoul Wallenberg, had already inspired me with his heroism. Now another man, Per Anger, had made me realize that each of us *can* make a difference. That evening my life was forever changed.

One Man Can
Make a Difference

Dim headlights shone through the late-night winter darkness, brightening as they approached the Eisner canal at Andau, close to Vienna. Pulling up near the edge of the black, murky water, the vehicle stopped. Out stepped a distinguished-looking man holding a slim pocket flashlight.

Above, a bare sliver of moonlight touched the sky as small rubber boats reached the shore. The man with the flashlight and a few others assisted the passengers—cold, hungry men, women, and children—out of the muddy water and headed them toward the hot soup and blankets stocked in the vehicle.

Briefly, the flashlight's tiny beam shone in the Swede's face.

"Per Anger! Per Anger! Do you remember me? You saved me once from the Nazis. This time you have saved me from the Russians," exclaimed a woman who recognized the Swede.

The year was 1956. Ten years after its liberation from Nazism, Hungary had revolted against the Soviet liberator-conqueror and its Communist government. The Soviet Union had been temporarily stunned but was not permanently defeated, and the brief period of freedom provided in the Hungarian Uprising had swiftly ended as the superpower again swallowed the small nation.

Hundreds of Hungarians, some remembering their escape from the Nazis, had fled from the Russian troops and followed the Danube toward Vienna. There the river branched off into eight miles of canals. In small rubber boats, barely distinguishable from the dark water, students helped transport the refugees from one side of the canal to the other, where Per Anger and his assistants awaited. Many refugees were ill or dying when they came to shore.

The man now standing knee-deep in the icy water, the counselor to the Swedish embassy in Vienna, was making history repeat itself. Ten years before, Anger had begun to effect rescues, removing Jews from Nazi clutches.

It had started late one night in the spring of 1944, when Per Anger heard a light knock on the door of his Budapest home. Standing in the darkness outside, a man covered the yellow Jewish star on his chest with what looked like a passport. Shame and desperation were written on Hugo Wohl's face as he entered the room and the door closed behind him.

Because of the trade connections between Hungary and Sweden, Wohl and Anger had become good friends. A leading Jewish businessman, Wohl was director of a company called Svenska Tungsram Orion. Though the company's headquarters were in Budapest, business required him to travel between Sweden and Hungary twice a year. Since his travels had always required a visa, he had been in regular contact with Per Anger at the Swedish legation.

On this night, however, Wohl's visit was not related to trade. The man was desperate for his very life and that of his family.

"Per, now you must help me" were the first words out of Wohl's mouth.

For a moment, Anger hesitated, feeling the man's shame. Even today when Anger talks about the incident, it is obvious that the memory of seeing this good man, this friend, with his dignity stripped away is still painful.[1]

Then an idea began to come to him. Sweden routinely issued provisional passports to Swedish citizens who had lost theirs. These documents insured their passage to Sweden, where they would have to prove their citizenship. True, Wohl was not a Swedish citizen, but perhaps the passes could still be used.

Why not, thought Anger, *give a provisional passport to Hugo Wohl—and eventually to others?* Anger had no real authority to do this, and like Swedish minister Carl Ivan Danielsson (who in modern terms would have been called the ambassador of the Swedish embassy), Anger did not break rules. The correct career diplomat, Anger was reliable and kind, but until now he had done his job within the given guidelines. Facing a choice that would affect his own future and the lives of many others, would he break those rules?

"They can fire me," he finally said out loud. "But I have to do this." Hugo Wohl and his family received the first illegal provisional passports, and their lives were saved.[2]

Until 1944, Hungary had escaped the worst ravages of Hitler's war. Indeed, this nation's Jewish population, one million strong, represented the last large, intact group of Jews in Europe. With the destruction of the Hungarian Jews, Hitler's Final Solution—the Jewish genocide—would be nearly complete.

By 1944 it had become apparent to both sides that Hitler was losing the war. As a Wehrmacht corporal who had escaped on foot stated, "After Normandy, we had no illusions any more. We knew that we stood with our backs to the wall."[3] Hitler became aware that he could no longer trust the vacillations of Budapest's Horthy regime, which he had once seen as an ally. So the Reich gave up all pretense of leaving the Hungarian Jews in relative safety and focused on their annihilation. They were rounded up and transported to German camps, slated for extermination.

During the last nine months of World War II, the thirty-two-year-old second secretary in Budapest's Swedish legation defied this further attempt by Hitler to destroy the Jewish race. But Anger was not alone in his defiance of the Reich. In July 1944 another young Swede, Raoul Wallenberg, joined him. Wallenberg had been specifically sent to Budapest to aid the Jews, and under him the rescue plans escalated into a dimension unequaled in modern history.

On the German side, Anger and Wallenberg faced an antagonist who held a relatively low rank in the Nazi party. Nevertheless, the notorious Adolf Eichmann was a man of great power and determination.

One of history's greatest conflicts of wits would be played out on this battlefield in Budapest. Three men, Eichmann, Wallenberg, and Anger, would see their lives intertwine as they contested for Israel's destiny.

With the reversal in their relationship to the Reich, virtually overnight Hungary experienced the Nazi-enforced changes toward the Jews. One day, as Anger describes it, everything was as usual. Then on March 19, 1944, the Germans invaded Hungary. Shortly after, when Anger walked out on the streets of Budapest, multitudes of people wore bright yellow stars sewn upon their clothing. It marked them as Jews, outcasts, "life unworthy of life."

Anger remembers:

I will never forget the day the ordinances went into effect. One could see Budapest's Jews, that is, every third or fourth person one met, marked with the yellow star as a sign they belonged to a despised pariah class that had been doomed to destruction. Against the dark clothing most of them wore, the six-pointed stars of a poisonous cadmium yellow seemed luminous. Some bore them with the resignation of a thousand years of suffering, others were too proud to show themselves outdoors with this mark on their breasts. Some tried pathetically to hide their stars momentarily with briefcase, package, or purse, the way one hides a handicap. Of course, this, too, was punishable. German soldiers saw to it that the ordinances were obeyed, but the Hungarian Arrow Crossmen [the Hungarian Nazis], who willingly informed on those they knew, were even more dangerous.[4]

Another Swedish diplomat, Lars Berg, describes the scene with equal poignancy:

Below the window I could also see the long row of people waiting for admittance to the legation. They were not ordinary visitors, looking for business information or wanting to pay their cordial respects to the Swedish minister; they had come to plead for their lives—their own and those of their families. Their faces were pale as the yellow stars they were wearing sewn onto their jackets and coats. The yellow star was not worn as an adornment but as an enforced mark of disgrace. It seemed to cry out: "I am a Jew. Treat me as you like. Beat me; deport me; rob me; send me to the gas chamber. I am not a human being, just a Jew!"[5]

The sacred symbol of Judaism had been desecrated into an object of hate and destruction. It had become a sign of shame rather than a beacon of hope and pride. Throughout the war it marked out those who should die.

The star decree that the Nazis had long desired for the Jews of Hungary was put into effect on March 29, 1944. However, marking was not new in Hungary. As early as 1941, Jewish students in the Technical College of Budapest had "voluntarily" agreed to wear an insignia that set them apart from Aryan students.

The 1944 decree required all Jews above the age of six to wear a yellow Jewish star measuring four by six inches. Exemptions existed for certain war veterans. In addition, after considerable conflict with the Catholic Church because of the Catholic clergy's objections to the religious implications of the star, the day before the patch was required, Christian clergy, Jews in mixed marriages, and widows and orphans of World War II soldiers also received an exemption.[6]

Even the Jews who received provisional passports were not totally immune from the Nazi oppression. To protect them, the Swedes established safe houses, which always had a Swedish flag outside that distinguished them as Swedish territory. Eventually thirty-two of these apartments along the Danube housed at least twenty thousand Jews. As Anger put it, Sweden became the biggest landlord in Budapest. Outside the safe houses were posted Aryan-looking young Jews, dressed like Nazis.

Both the depth of the anti-Semitism instilled in German soldiers and Anger's innate diplomatic skills are illustrated in Lars Berg's account of one attack on a safe house. A group of Nazis had taken it over, and Anger and several others were called to the scene by Mrs. Forgo, a Swedish woman married to a Hungarian with some Jewish blood in his ancestry.

According to Berg:

Anger explained to them that they were in a house under the protection of the Swedish legation and that they had to leave at once. The Germans' first reaction seemed to be to throw Anger and us out into the street. . . . But there was something resolute in the appearance of those three Swedes . . . that made them hesitate. One of the Germans grabbed his tommy gun. We released the safety catches on the automatics in our pockets. The situation was tense. But the gun was lowered again.

The Germans admitted that they knew they were in a Swedish house. But the owner was a Jew and as such naturally without any legal rights. Furthermore they were going to arrest him on the following morning and have him deported for not wearing the yellow star.

In a very gentle manner Anger explained to the German soldiers that a Swedish Jew was by no means without legal rights and that Hungarian Jews with Swedish protective passports did not have to wear any yellow star.

"Do you really mean that the Jews in Sweden do not wear any yellow star and that you consider them to be just like any other people?" The young misguided boys were flabbergasted.

Meanwhile Mrs. Forgo had whispered to Anger in Swedish that her husband had managed to escape. In order to avoid trouble, the Germans could stay in the house overnight. Still controlling the situation superbly, Anger told the soldiers that they would be allowed to stay where they were till next morning if they behaved decently. If they did not leave then, he would report them to their officer in command for having broken into a Swedish house.

Anger gave his orders in a calm and firm manner. To our great relief, the Germans nodded assent.

Mrs. Forgo later on reported to the legation that the Germans had behaved extremely well after our departure. They had left the following morning, never to come back.[7]

Persecution is not new to the Jewish people, but the Holocaust has been one particularly outstanding and horrible example of that persecution. Yet history has proven that the oppression of any people often becomes the platform upon which heroes are developed. In the case of the Jews, those heroes are sometimes other Jews, and sometimes they are what we have come to call Righteous Gentiles.

Centuries ago, the bravery of Esther, a Jewish woman married to King Xerxes, was described in the Bible. When his wicked counselor, Haman, tricked the king into agreeing to a plan to kill all Jews, Queen Esther intervened, despite the very real possibility that the king would kill her for her actions. For to approach the king without being summoned carried with it the possibility of death. Nevertheless Esther approached the king, and through her persuasion saved many Jewish lives.

Raul Hilberg comments, "In exile the Jews had always been a minority; they had always been in danger; but they had learned that they could avert danger and survive destruction by placating and appeasing their enemies. Even in ancient Persia an appeal by Queen Esther was more effective than the mobilization of an army."[8]

But now German armies were being mobilized against the Jews, and there could be no appeasement. In many cases, their safety lay in the hands of people who were willing to risk their lives for others. Some *were* willing to take up the challenge.

When the Nazis had invaded Holland earlier in World War II, Casper ten Boom, an elderly Dutch watchmaker who has also been declared a "Righteous Gentile," had every reason not to become involved. He had just celebrated the one hundredth birthday of the family business, his family loved him, and the community respected him. But after the Nazi takeover, the ten Boom family became involved with the Dutch resistance, and their home became a hiding place for Jews.

One evening a clergyman brought a watch to the ten Booms for repair. He was a friend of the devout Christian family, so Casper's daughter Corrie asked him to take in a Jewish baby whose parents were about to be arrested. When she showed him the hidden child, the clergyman's alarm was immediate. Corrie remembered:

> For a moment I saw compassion and fear struggle in his face. Then he straightened. "No. Definitely not. We could lose our lives for that Jewish child!"
>
> Unseen by either of us, Father had appeared in the doorway. "Give the child to me, Corrie," he said.
>
> Father held the baby close, his white beard brushing its cheek, looking into the little face with eyes as blue and innocent as the baby's own. At last he looked up at the pastor. "You say we could lose our lives for this child. I would consider that the greatest honor that could come to my family."[9]

Because he took such action, the gentle old man's life would end in violence, at the hands of Nazi thugs.

Psychiatrist Dr. Viktor Frankl, a survivor of the Nazi camps, once said something to the effect that some found God in the Holocaust while others lost him. It could be added that some, like Per Anger, became heroes, while for others the Holocaust became a platform for failure and cowardice.

It was all based on each person's choice.

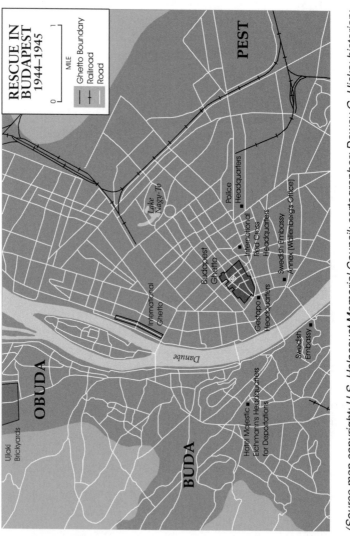

RESCUE IN
BUDAPEST
1944–1945

0 MILE

— Ghetto Boundary
—+— Railroad
—— Road

Uljaki
Brickyards

OBUDA

BUDA

Hotel Majestic
Eichmann's Headquarters
for Deportations

Danube

International
Ghetto

*Lake
Nagy-Tó*

Budapest
Ghetto

International
Red Cross
Headquarters

Gestapo
Headquarters

Swedish Embassy
Annex (Wallenberg's Office)

Swedish
Embassy

Police
Headquarters

PEST

Per Anger in a park in Göteberg, Sweden, at the age of two. *(Courtesy of Per Anger family.)*

Per Anger's parents, Elsa and David Anger, on their golden wedding anniversary 1962 in Stockholm. *(Courtesy of Per Anger family.)*

Lieutenant Per Anger, Royal
Swedish Lifeguards, 1941.
(Courtesy of Per Anger family.)

Per Anger in Berlin, 1940, on
his first diplomatic mission.
(Courtesy of Per Anger family.)

The Royal Swedish Embassy (or Legation, as it was called at that time) on Gellért Hill in Budapest. *(Courtesy of Per Anger family.)*

Per Anger on the top of the Royal Swedish Legation Building in the Spring of 1943. *(Courtesy of Per Anger family.)*

A happy Per Anger, engaged to be married, Stockholm, February 1943.
(Courtesy of Per Anger family.)

Per Anger hunting small game in Transylvania in 1943. *(Courtesy of Per Anger family.)*

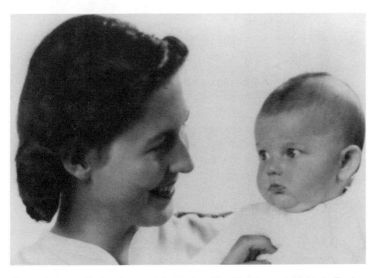

Elena Anger with the Angers' first baby, Birgitta, August 1944, in Budapest. *(Photographer: Paul Veres. Courtesy of Per Anger family.)*

Minister Danielsson, head of the Swedish legation in Budapest throughout the war years. *(Photographer: Elena Anger. Courtesy of Per Anger family.)*

Attache Per Anger with Valdemar Langlet, the Swedish Red Cross delegate who stayed on to help. *(Courtesy of Per Anger family.)*

Swedish diplomat Lars Berg with his dog, which was later taken from him by the Russian soldiers. *(Courtesy of Per Anger family.)*

A passport picture of Hugo Wohl, who worked directly under Wallenberg on the Pest side of Budapest. *(Courtesy of the Wohl-Ernster family.)*

Thomas Veres, Wallenberg's official photographer. Veres was introduced to Wallenberg by Anger and provided a pictorial record of the events in Budapest. *(Photographer: Thomas Veres. Courtesy of Thomas Veres.)*

Thomas Veres in Budapest with his camera. *(Photographer: Thomas Veres. Courtesy of Thomas Veres.)*

Preparation for Conflict

I n the south of Stockholm, on Christmas Eve 1921, two boys anxiously awaited Father Christmas. Outside the Anger home, the snow lay in high drifts and the air was bitter cold. Inside the house nestled below the mountains, Per and his brother Jan felt the excitement of that special night—the most important one for a Swedish child.

From their upstairs window, the boys could see a long way over the white, quiet countryside. They could hear their father downstairs preparing to leave, and each boy wondered why he always was called away to work on Christmas Eve. The outside door closed after their father shouted a quick good-bye.

As usual, their Christmas Eve dinner had been festive and special. The aroma of ham blended with the smell of the coffee cake's yeast and cardamom and lingered in the air, reminding the boys of the smorgasbord feast. Potato sausage, sylta, lutefisk, and various cheeses combined to form the memory of yet another happy Christmas Eve.

The evening was getting late. Tomorrow the family would get up at 4:30 A.M. to go to Julotta for the annual church Christmas program. Still there had been no presents, no Father Christmas. Even their father had seemed to abandon the possibility of further festivities by going to work.

Suddenly the boys saw Father Christmas himself, coming around the old stable in the yard. With great effort he struggled through the snowdrifts, at times almost losing his balance. The boys held their breath in anticipation. Across his back lay a huge bag filled with packages. The heavy load swayed as the jolly man struggled through the soft, fluffy snow.

As he disappeared from view, the boys waited quietly. Next they heard a loud knock on the door downstairs. Father Christmas read a poem in a loud, booming voice. It was about gifts being brought for the children, whose mother had vouched for their goodness in a letter she had written to Father Christmas. The boys heard the gifts being removed from the big bag and deposited in the house.

They knew it would not do to run downstairs yet—not while Father Christmas was still there. That might ruin everything. Quietly they waited, the tension mounting to an almost unbearable pitch.

The front door opened again, and their mother's glad voice greeted their father. He had not worked as long as the boys feared he might.

"I'm so sorry I missed you, Father Christmas," they heard their father say. "I was called out unexpectedly to work." Father Christmas replied with an indistinguishable mumble.

"Would you like some coffee?" their father continued. The clatter of cups followed, and the boys knew this would take still more time. *Why do adults always have to stop for coffee?* they wondered.

Finally Father Christmas left, clumping in his heavy boots, struggling through the snowdrifts, back around the stable, disappearing with his empty bag.

"Per, Jan," their father called a few minutes later from downstairs. "Come down! Father Christmas has just been here. I met him when I came home."

Still full of their faith in the miracle of Father Christmas, the boys tumbled down the stairs. Early in the morning, on Christmas Day, they would remember the divine baby in the manger and worship. But tonight the presents lay before them, heaped under the pine tree. Its white candles lit the room, and outside the stars seemed brighter, while the moon cast its light across the glistening snow. This was now truly Christmas Eve, night of all nights.[1]

Because of his happy childhood memories, celebrations like Christmas and traditions in general were always important to Per Anger. One day those cheerful traditions would become even more important—in the hard times of the war years they buffered stress and gave him stability in the midst of chaos.

On a very different Christmas Eve twenty-three years later, as the Reich was losing its grip on Europe, Per Anger's wife and child awaited him in Sweden. In contrast to that boyhood Christmas, Anger spent the day under dangerous circumstances in Hungary. The Nazis had been essentially defeated by the Allies and Budapest was being overtaken by the Russians. The members of the Swedish legation were trying to evade the Russian conflict with the Germans.

For the last nine months of 1944, since the Germans had occupied Hungary, Anger's position as second secretary to the Swedish legation in Budapest had unofficially included a role in the final struggle to save the Jews of Budapest. To save these people, the legation had remained

35

in Budapest, despite the dangers of the imminent Allied invasion. The legation's work was not yet done.

However, war had not stopped the plans for a traditional Swedish Christmas celebration. On December 23, two of the Swedish diplomats, Göte Carlsson and Lars Berg, had decided to stay in their own house so that they could prepare a big Christmas party for the Swedish legation. It was a dangerous decision. The Hungarian Nazis (also called the Nyilas or Arrow Cross), who roamed freely about the city, were ruthless. The Swedes could not even count on using their neutrality as a defense, because the Nyilas had less regard for their position than did the German Nazis. Yet since they were armed, the two Swedes felt reasonably protected.

Through the late night they wrote poems on all the packages, according to Swedish tradition. These added humor and mystique to each gift, giving little hints as to the package's contents and what the recipient might use it for.

After finishing the packages, Carlsson and Berg instructed the cook on the preparation of rice porridge. Then the huge tree, which had been obtained from someone working directly with Wallenberg, was decorated. By 4:00 A.M., all was ready for the celebration. Christmas Eve would be a reprieve from the raging storm that whirled around these people, who had seen so much hate and destruction.

At 6:00 A.M. the telephone rang. The Finnish legation asked Berg for help, announcing it had been attacked by the Arrow Cross. A call to the Swedish legation informed Berg that the same attack had been made there before it happened at the Finnish legation. Berg called Per Anger, warning him not to go to the legation; another call told Berg that two women from the Swedish legation, Margareta Bauer, a secretary, and Asta Nilsson, the Red Cross representative, had already been captured.

Later that day, Lars Berg was taken by the Arrow Cross. He knew the Arrow Cross had little or no respect for neutral nations, but it would be different if he could obtain German protection. The Germans were very predictable in their slavish obedience to orders and their attempt to treat neutral countries properly. Through an incredible stroke of luck, combined with clever, fast thinking, he managed to get to a German officer. His hunch had been right. Not knowing Berg's rank, but fearing not to obey him in case he was important, the German got rid of the Arrow Cross. At the end of the incident, Berg received papers putting him under German protection. These proved temporarily valuable, until the preponderance of Russian power in the city made it wise for Berg to destroy the papers.

On Christmas Eve, the Soviet troops began their siege of Budapest. The battle would rage hotly through Christmas Day. Though the Germans made an effort to defend the city, the Soviets had taken the German garrison by surprise. Assessing his situation, the German commander requested permission from Hitler to surrender the city. Hitler replied with a flat denial. The siege would continue into the New Year. Then when the Soviets finally entered the city, the so-called liberators destroyed property, plundered, looted, and raped. On January 16, the Pest part of Budapest was "liberated." Four days later an armistice agreement was reached, and on February 13 the Buda side was taken over by the Soviet forces.

Returning to his house early Christmas Eve afternoon, Berg found that the Arrow Cross had raided the house, and the presents with the carefully written poems were gone. The whole house had been ransacked, and the only intact object was the still magnificent Christmas tree, standing in the midst of the disorder.

In spite of the chaos, for a brief time Berg had what he needed to make his escape from Budapest with reasonable safety. Ironically, his best Christmas gift had been that German protective pass. Yet he could not leave without knowing that his fellow diplomats were also safe.

Some instinct led Berg to visit the office of a man who seemed inclined to help Wallenberg. Perhaps, Berg thought, there he might find Per Anger. Arriving, he found Anger's car parked outside. Inside, to his joy, he found both Anger and Wallenberg.

A little while later, Berg left the room, returning with two bottles of champagne. They drank to each other's health and to a merry Christmas. Though their celebration wasn't very Swedish, it was Christmas Eve, and they were safe for the moment.

Later that evening, they found Minister Danielsson. The two captured Swedish women had been safely rescued, and Christmas Eve ended with a true sense of peace that contrasted with the danger of all that could have been.

The next day the Swedish legation celebrated Christmas Day with the Swiss chargé d'affaires, who offered them some coffee. The candles on the tree at Lars Berg's house were never lit, and the feast was never eaten; but Christmas did bring a temporary respite from the horrors around them.[2]

For Per Anger it was only the second Christmas since his marriage, and already he and his wife, Elena, were separated by many miles and a war. The previous Christmas, Christmas 1943, had been their first Christmas together. Along with the staff in Hungary, they had obtained some food through the diplomatic mail. The highlight of the celebration had been chocolate bars, which they had divided among themselves. It too had not been a traditional Swedish Christmas, but at least the couple had been together.

The man who spent the first two Christmases of his marriage in a war-torn country had been born in the peaceful town of Göteborg, Sweden, on December 7, 1913. There Per Johan Valentin Anger had been baptized into the Lutheran Church. Per would be the eldest of three boys, all raised in the southern part of Stockholm.

His mother, Elsa, an English and French teacher, had first met her husband, David, in Göteborg. They were married there in 1912. Elsa had studied in England and had a strong appreciation of English culture. She passed her love of literature on to Per, who, while he was studying law at the university, envied his friends who could study poems and essays.

In 1916 the Anger family moved to Stockholm. David Anger was an engineer with important responsibilities in the construction of bridges, streets, and other public projects. He was a quiet man, but behind his lack of words lay a strong personality with deep feelings.

In Stockholm the family lived in a large house at the foot of a hill in the southern part of the city. Most of the people who lived there were not well off. Living conditions were fairly primitive, and the family had to carry in water from the outside and use an old heating stove, of a type that was prevalent throughout Sweden.

Per has always felt that his school experience was vital to what he did with the rest of his life. After studying for three years at the local primary school, he attended high school with boys from many different backgrounds. Per graduated at nineteen.

The Angers' family life was warm and loving, and even as a child Per deeply respected his parents' hardworking approach to life. Furthermore, the mountains, the snow, and the abundance of nature provided an ideal environment for raising children.

Per's brother Jan was five years younger than he, while his youngest brother, Claes, was thirteen years his junior. Per shared his childhood largely with Jan, climbing the mountains, skiing, and doing what children do as they grow.

A difficult experience that became a formative influence on Per's early life was his bout with tuberculosis, a disease that was rampant in the early twentieth century.

At age seven or eight, Per contracted a light case of the disease in his lungs. Exhibiting great ingenuity, Per's father constructed a heat-radiating lamp. At a time when so many methods failed to treat the disease, the lamp worked, and Per completely recovered.

In 1925, a few years after Per recovered from his illness, Sweden officially disarmed in the naive notion that war was passé. To young Per this policy came as a disappointment. The idea of being a great warrior very much appealed to him, as it does to many boys. Indeed, at that time Per felt convinced he wanted to be a military person. The warrior kings of Swedish history and prominent military heroes of other countries had become his boyhood heroes. The idea of commanding people, while operating as part of a team that shared camaraderie, appealed to Per. Above all, he wanted to help people. The desire was so strong that at one time his mother thought he might become a priest or a pastor.

As a result of these goals, when he was twelve Per, and later his brother Jan, joined the Home Guard where they learned about defending their country. This exercise involved considerable physical exertion, and Per built up his tuberculosis-weakened body.

Most of Per's childhood was happy, and the pleasantness of those years probably gave him the sense of security that he would later need during difficult war experiences and for the rest of his life.

Just as Christmas was full of tradition, so the family had a pleasant balance of play and work. The two intermingled with predictable events that the family anticipated with joy. For example, on birthdays, in the morning a tray would be brought in with a cake that displayed a number of candles matching the age of the birthday person. A wish was made, and it was expected to come true if all the candles were blown out with one breath. For a child, juice would be on the tray; adults always received coffee. Of course there were packages to open. Such times provided predictable enjoyment and structure to life. Even the time of day at which the birthday was celebrated could be counted on.

After he had finished school in 1933, Per Anger became an officer in the reserve, which focused on the defense of Sweden. He spent one year in cadet school and then, during the summer of 1934, became a corporal in his regiment. That fall he first went to the University of Stockholm and thereafter to the University of Uppsala, where in 1939 he graduated with a degree in law.

When Per was twenty-three and Jan eighteen, Jan became a pilot in the Swedish Air Force. On his first solo flight, Jan's plane went into a tailspin, which forced him to jump. By the time he jumped, he was too low for the parachute to open. Jan's death in 1936 was the greatest tragedy the family endured, and his parents never fully recovered from it.

To Per it was a never-to-be-forgotten event, but his brother's death also became a challenge to him. Because he died while serving his country, Jan became a role model. *What is good for my country?* or *What is my duty to my country?* has always been a paramount question in Per Anger's decision making.

As he was studying law, Anger realized that the subject did not have a very strong appeal for him. Determined to finish what he had started, he also felt the study of law would open doors for him in the future. He became interested in becoming a diplomat. After speaking to his mother's cousin, who was in the foreign office, he began to feel that perhaps through this he could help people as he had always wanted to do.

Then history took its own turn. In 1939 Hitler invaded Poland and war broke out. Because he was in the reserves, Anger was drafted and commanded to stay in Stockholm to defend the city. He had just taken his last university course, which happened to be in criminal law, but was not yet slated to take his law exam.

As time went on Anger realized that he was beginning to forget the finer details of his law studies. Worried that if he waited much longer he might not pass the final test, he contacted his professor, told him of his dilemma, and asked if he could take the test immediately. Anger is sure that he was given an easier exam because he appeared in full military dress to take his test—the professor was a great admirer of the military. He is equally sure that the hand of God led him in this as well as other affairs of his life that went so remarkably well. He passed the exam, and his anxieties were relieved.

After Anger returned to his regiment, where he was a lieutenant, an offer came from the foreign office to serve in Berlin. However, Finland had just gone to war with the Soviet Union in a territorial battle, and in 1939 there were appeals for Swedish volunteers to fight in support of Finland. Anger had to make a crucial choice. In which direction did his duty lie? To go and fight for Finland seemed courageous. Yet he was also needed by the foreign office in Berlin.

In the long scope of things, he reasoned, he might do more for his country if he took this chance to unofficially enter the foreign service. Then, after Berlin, Anger could return to Sweden and take the official test to become a diplomat. He decided to go to Berlin, where he stayed for a year and a half before returning to Sweden to officially begin a lifetime of service for his country as a diplomat. In this role he would travel all over the world under a variety of conditions.[3]

Anger arrived in Berlin by train on February 1, 1940. He introduced himself to his immediate superior, the counselor of trade, Torsten Vinell, on the coldest winter day within memory.

Anger's main duties involved taking care of trade matters on the grassroots level, a task that was not as ordinary as it sounds. The major negotiations concerned selling iron ore to the Germans in return for the ability to buy as much of their coal as possible. Maintaining a delicate balance was the key. Sweden needed coal, but if she shipped too much iron ore to the Germans, it would jeopardize her neutral stance with the Allies.

As the youngest member of the Swedish legation, Anger also had the job of sending coded messages to the Ministry of Foreign Affairs in Stockholm. One Sunday at the end of March 1940, while Anger was on call at home, he received a message ordering him to go immediately to the legation to send a very important coded message.

When Anger arrived at the legation, he found the department heads gathered, looking somber and tense. In due time Mr. Vinell entered Anger's office and informed him that in a few minutes he would receive a message of extreme importance, which Anger would then send. Tension mounted. Finally the message came. Intelligence sources reported a German plan for the invasion of Norway and Denmark. These sources did not know if Sweden was also included in that plan, but it was certainly possible. The invasion was to be part of an overall plan to conquer all of western Europe.

Anger was dependent upon a big, clumsy ciphering machine in order to send his messages, which only added to the challenge of the task. Luckily Anger had the help of a deputy military attaché, and together they managed to get the machine to function properly. Every now and then someone would check to see if they were done with the job. Eventually, in spite of the idiosyncrasies of the machine, they finished. Then Anger walked out into the quietness of the Berlin night to the post office, where he mailed the message to Stockholm.

Upon returning home, a terrific fear overwhelmed him: *What if we did something wrong when we set the code and no one can read it in Stockholm?* he asked himself. Then, wrote Anger many years later, "The Germans will invade at dawn, and in all the history books it will state that Sweden was not warned ahead of time because of negligence by an attaché in Berlin. As a result I could not sleep a wink that night. Luckily, the message had been understood."[4] Ironically, in contrast to Anger's concern, when the message was received, the foreign office was not worried and felt the personnel at the Swedish legation in Berlin must indeed be very nervous. Even their Danish and Norwegian colleagues in Berlin did not believe the intelligence data.

In Stetten a Swedish seamen's pastor was asked to count the number of ships docked in the harbor, waiting to be used in the invasion. After the answer came back, on April 4, 1940, a last warning was sent to Stockholm. This time the seriousness of the situation became apparent, and some desperate, if insufficient, efforts were made to strengthen the Swedish defense. The Norwegians were also alerted, but they did not believe the warning was valid.

By radio the members of the Swedish legation in Berlin followed the frightening events of the next days. Copenhagen was invaded, and on April 9 Norway was attacked. While Norway was ultimately occupied by the Nazis, there was heroic resistance. The fort in Oslo was manned by one officer with a few men who had one rusty cannon at their disposal. According to the rules of the fort, the cannon could be used if an unexpected foreign warship entered Norwegian waters. As darkness began to fall, the Norwegians saw the contours of a big warship approaching. The Norwegian officer ordered the cannon fired with the only cannonball available. Fortunately, their aim was excellent. The approaching German cruiser, *Blücher,* sank with a thousand men on board. This incident gave the Norwegians some warning, and as a result, the king and the government of Norway were able to evacuate. The Danes, however, had no warning. From here on the war continued to escalate, with the Netherlands, Belgium, and France all invaded with lightning speed.

Many European countries responded slowly to the rapidly growing threat of Adolf Hitler; meanwhile, in Berlin he was treated as a god. During May 1940, the soldiers who had taken Paris returned to Berlin. The Germans shouted enthusiastically in the streets and threw flowers at the soldiers' feet. Many in the crowd probably felt the war was over. People gathered in huge crowds at the Wilhelmsplatz, where Hitler often spoke from the balcony.

Standing in the crowd was Per Anger. With his usual appropriateness he wore a hat, and in general he just blended in with the crowd. When Hitler came out on the balcony and talked to the people, whom he mesmerized with his strident rhetoric and imposing presence, suddenly the man behind Anger struck his head so violently that Anger's hat flew off. Anger had overlooked one rule of protocol: When one was eye to eye with the Führer, one was not allowed to wear a hat.[5]

During the course of his diplomatic career, which had only just begun in Berlin, Anger encountered dangers and challenges that extended well beyond the expected liabilities of foreign service. The ordinary life of a diplomat, even under peacetime conditions, however, is not that of idleness and purposeless amusement. Speaking of those who imagine that diplomats spend their lives on golf courses and at cocktail parties, Lars Berg points out that anyone who thinks that way should rise early and watch the cars line up in front of an embassy while the rest of the city is fast asleep. Furthermore, anyone who takes part in business travel and entertaining will tell you that the tension involved in these activities makes many people quit for a less lucrative job that allows them more free time and relaxation.

Per Anger was not working in peacetime conditions, yet according to his colleagues, he was the one who kept their spirits up; he was the one who maintained his sense of humor.[6] Anger dealt with the unusual stress that comes with such a position by returning to the things that meant much to him in childhood. Speaking on Swedish radio a few years ago, Anger referred to the book *Safety Zones,* which defines a *safety zone* as a person, place, thing, or belief that comforts and refurbishes one in going on.[7] In defining his own safety zones, Anger explained:

> For me it has been a place. Very often when I'm home, when I'm back in Sweden, I go back to the place where we grew up as children. There was a big house, just on the outskirts of Stockholm, on a big mountain where we always played and enjoyed ourselves with the neighbor children. Very often I go there and sort of meditate. I think back on my happy childhood and how I feel in the presence of my parents and how I still feel their support.[8]

For Anger, growing up in Sweden was a time of nurturing and preparation for a life that was to have an enormous impact on the lives of hundreds of Jews.

3

Inside the
Swedish Legation

I n August of 1944, four years after his arrival in Berlin, young diplomat Per Anger traveled home to Sweden from Budapest. During his brief visit he had a lengthy lunch with Iver Olsen of the American embassy in Sweden and updated him on recent events in Budapest.

Some fifty years later, while going through some files in Stockholm, Anger found a letter from Olsen to the United States State Department that described that conversation: "I had lunch with the . . . Secretary of the Swedish Legation in Budapest [Per Anger], who is here for a short while. He is a fine chap and had many interesting comments to make. He said Wallenberg is working very hard and doing everything possible, which items he has also emphasized to the Foreign Office."[1] The letter goes on to describe Anger's general assessment of the best way to protect the Jews and the attitude of the Hungarian government toward them.

Olsen also described Anger's original reactions to what he heard about atrocities being done to the Jews of Hun-

47

gary—atrocities Anger felt he could not take on hearsay. He must know with absolute certainty that these events had indeed taken place and not depend on rumors.

In one instance, to be an eyewitness, Anger went to a brick factory where ten thousand Jews had been herded into so small an area that they were forced to stand up, closely packed together. This went on for five days, during which they remained without any sanitary facilities. Even old people and children were packed together with the rest. Anger saw eighty human beings at a time being counted out precisely and loaded into boxcars, after which the doors were nailed shut. Many died standing.

According to Olsen's document, which was only declassified by the United States State Department in 1972, Anger went on to tell about teenage girls of only fourteen or fifteen who were literally kidnapped off the streets of Budapest. They were taken to other areas where they were temporarily confined. The words *war whore* were tattooed on their arms, and they were shipped to places as far away as Hamburg to be used sexually until they were no longer usable. Many of the girls came from cultured and protected backgrounds. They were not at all streetwise, and were especially ill equipped for lives of forced prostitution.[2]

For Anger such discoveries were an abrupt start to what was to become an unusually challenging diplomatic career in which the hands-on approach he showed in Budapest would become an outstanding characteristic.

Yet to understand this hero in Budapest, one must comprehend more fully the road to Budapest. In spite of the very active diplomatic function he performed in Berlin, Per Anger's official career in the Swedish foreign office really began after his time in Berlin. Following his return to Sweden from Germany, he had to pass the examination for the foreign office. Of this period of his life he once said, "God helped me."

The test to enter foreign service was reputed to be difficult. One needed to be knowledgeable about Swedish history and the Swedish social system. A knowledge of foreign languages was also important. Anger had studied French and German extensively, but he felt less sure of his French. His time in Berlin had been helpful in developing his skill in German. It was therefore fortunate that when he went to the foreign office for the exam in language, they decided to emphasize German.

After taking the test, Anger was sent to the head of the administration for approval. If this man recommended him, it was more or less a sure thing that he would be admitted to the foreign service. On the other hand, if this man decided against an applicant, that person had no recourse. For Anger, the end result of the interview was influenced by his answer to just one question.

Although he was now a Swedish citizen, the head diplomat was of Polish extraction. Hitler had just taken Poland by force so, of course, the man hated the Germans. On this particular day, when Anger went to his home for his interview, the old man was not feeling well. When his daughter opened the door, she warned Per: "I am so sorry, but my father has very bad lumbago today. He is in much pain." Anger knew the importance of those next few minutes and realized that something as unplanned as lumbago could ruin his chances for a lifelong career.

As the older man walked into the room, it was apparent that he was in severe pain. He walked stiffly and could scarcely move. Fortunately Anger knew about the man's hatred for the Germans, so he was somewhat prepared for what happened next. The first question was: "Anger, do you think the Germans are going to win this war?"

At this time Hitler had already taken much of Europe. One had to be very optimistic to believe that Hitler would lose the war. Therefore, the question was a difficult one to answer satisfactorily. With innate diplomacy Anger replied: "Sir, I am inexperienced, so I don't feel that I can give you an accurate answer to a question like that. But before I left Berlin I interviewed our military attaché, a very wise colonel who knows world politics and who knows the Russians. I asked him the same question. He said that there was not a chance that Hitler was going to win this war."

The older man became more animated and exclaimed: "Did he really say that? How wonderful!" A case of lumbago had probably been helped, and most certainly a diplomatic career had been launched.

Commenting philosophically about this event more than fifty years later, Anger said: "I don't think that this was some sort of pure coincidence. . . . At that time you just thought it was natural, that you were just clever, and you had good luck. . . . But in the perspective of the years, when you look back on this series of events, you can see how you have been helped to come into the right path."[3]

Paralleling the period when Anger was developing his career plans and making his decision to enter the foreign service, he was also making some decisions in his personal life. As previously explained, it was essential for anyone who wanted to enter the foreign service to become fluent in French as well as German. Therefore, in the summer of 1938 Anger had gone to France and had lived with a French family in order to study and practice the language. On the way home to Stockholm, while he waited for a train in Hamburg, Anger had seen a young girl waiting with a man who appeared to be her grandfather. (Later he discovered that the gentleman was her Swiss uncle.) She was saying good-bye to him following her summer of studies in languages in Italy. Her name was Elena Wikstrom.

Like Per, Elena came from Stockholm, Sweden. When Per got into the train and found his compartment, there was a nurse sitting in front of him. In came the porter with the young girl's luggage. When the porter discovered that the nurse was getting off at the next stop, he asked the nurse to go to another compartment and gave the compartment to Elena, who was also going all the way to Stockholm.

Per thought that Elena was French or Russian, so he spoke to her in French. Finally she laughed and said: "Couldn't we just as easily speak Swedish?" That was the start of their acquaintance.

Elena had been brought up in a very strict home. She was not allowed to travel unchaperoned, with the present exception, because it was the last part of a journey and the distance was not great. Another stipulation of her upbringing was that she was never to loan money to a strange gentleman. Ordinarily Per would not have borrowed money from a strange woman. But suddenly, when the conductor came to collect the tickets, Per had no ticket! He turned his pockets inside out and searched his luggage. No ticket. He did not have enough money for a new ticket, so in desperation he asked Elena for money. By pooling their resources, they paid for his ticket. When they reached Stockholm, Per found his ticket deep down in a crease between the seats of the train.

As they neared the end of the journey, Per said: "Could I invite you to the cinema some day?" Elena explained that even though she was eighteen, she was not allowed to just go out with someone she met. At that time she lived on an island in the archipelago of Stockholm and was not allowed to receive guests there or to go into the city alone.

Patience and persistence, however, have always been two of Per's strong points. As time passed he managed to see her once or twice. Then he was transferred to Berlin in 1940, after finishing his studies and passing his law exam. Still Per persisted in the relationship, and their correspondence extended over a period of five years. On June 7, 1943, Per and Elena were married in Stockholm.[4]

Earlier Per had been appointed second secretary to the Swedish legation in Budapest, Hungary. He was now an official career diplomat. So after their wedding, the couple went back to Budapest for their honeymoon, where Per would continue his work.

When Per and Elena arrived in Budapest, they rented a house on Gellert Hill that had belonged to Baron Alfonse Weiss. Weiss was a part of the family that owned the Manfred-Weiss factories on Csepel Island, between Buda and Pest. He was looked upon as one of the wealthiest and most influential of the Jews of Budapest.

Later, when Anger heard rumors that the Jewish couple who had lived earlier in the Weiss home had been caught in the first wave of arrests, characteristically he went to the outskirts of Budapest to see for himself if they were in a German camp that had been erected there. The rumor was true and, as Anger put it in his book, "This was my first confrontation with the Nazi executioner state. . . . We became witnesses to something we had not thought possible in modern times: the beginning of a systematic extermination of a whole race."[5]

In Budapest, however, life still went on with some normalcy. The Angers took part in some hunting trips in a countryside that was rich in wild game. While Per was not an enthusiastic hunter, the sport supplemented their rationed diet. An occasional rabbit, for example, provided a welcome diversion from the ordinary daily diet.

In the months before the Nazi invasion, there was still a healthy cultural exchange between Sweden and Hungary. Visits to the opera or a sports event with other diplomats or leaders in trade and industry were not uncommon for the newlyweds. Much of the Swedish legation's work was still related to trade between Sweden and Hungary, so as in any business venture, socializing and developing good relationships fostered increased trade.

The avenue of trade between Sweden and Hungary first familiarized Raoul Wallenberg with that country. Working as a representative for a Swedish firm, the Central European Trading Company, Wallenberg had visited Hungary on numerous occasions. These trips enabled Wallenberg and the Angers to further develop a friendship that had begun long ago as an acquaintanceship in Sweden. The social times linked together by the interests in trade between the two countries provided a basis of familiarity and trust that would later help in the rescue efforts.

On July 9, 1944, Raoul Wallenberg was designated as a Swedish diplomat and sent to Budapest to save the last remaining intact group of Jews in Europe. Wallenberg came not only to save helpless people; he came to save a nation. Wallenberg, Anger, and Eichmann, the main players in the conflict over the Jews in Budapest, were all in the city.

Wallenberg's "appointment as secretary of the Swedish legation in Budapest was the indirect consequence of an action originally taken by President Roosevelt." American Jews had been anxious to help the Jews of Europe, and both the Jewish Agency Rescue Committee and the War Refugee Board in Washington had tried to give aid and rescue; but since the United States did not have an embassy in Budapest, it could do little. President Roosevelt initiated an appeal to neutral Sweden, and the result was the appointment of Raoul Wallenberg to the Swedish legation in Budapest to save the Jews of Hungary.[6]

This work combined Wallenberg's forthright action with Anger's diplomacy. By the time Wallenberg arrived in the summer of 1944, Per Anger's provisional passes had already saved the lives of many Jewish business leaders who had Swedish connections. Per and others in the legation had also developed good relationships with other neutral legations, but Wallenberg would intensify the mission to save Jewish lives.

It was important to separate Wallenberg from the location of the Swedish legation. In this way, for the safety of all involved, the appearance of neutrality could be maintained and the success of his work could be secured. The Swedish legation's right to continue to function during wartime and the permission for Wallenberg to stay in Budapest and rescue Jews depended largely on this facade of neutrality.

The two parts of Budapest, Buda and Pest, are naturally divided by the Danube River. On the one side of the river is Pest, where many businesses are located, while the more mountainous Buda houses the wealthy in beautiful mansions and accommodates the greater number of foreign embassies and legations. The Swedish legation was located in Buda. Therefore, Wallenberg moved his operation to the Pest side and opened up what was called Department B of the Swedish legation. Through the establishment of a separate section, Wallenberg, along with the people who assisted him—ultimately numbering over four hundred—was less hampered by the restrictions on the legation.

One of Wallenberg's assistants, Yngve Ekmark, was a Swedish consul who had stopped by to visit Budapest on his way home from Yugoslavia. When Ekmark saw he was needed, he didn't leave. He had a business background, so he became head of what they called the economic or commercial section of Wallenberg's operation. Ekmark provided food for the safe houses. This required making expeditions into the countryside to buy enormous quantities of meat, potatoes, and other foods and delivering these supplies to the safe houses.

Thomas Veres was another remarkable addition to this group of people who made a difference in the lives of so many. Introduced to Wallenberg by Per Anger, Veres was the son of Berta and Paul Veres. Paul Veres was a society photographer whose services were sought by people like Admiral Miklós Horthy and by those in diplomatic service. Thus, when Per Anger's first child was born in Budapest, the couple went to Paul Veres for pictures.

Along with his own innate creative talent, young Tom Veres had learned his photographic skills from his father. These skills were now to be used to record a pictorial history of the events in Budapest. Thus both written reports and a multitude of photographs would preserve a record for the world of the attempted genocide of the Jews of Hungary as well as the valiant efforts of the rescuers.

Taking pictures in public was at this point illegal in Hungary. One method Veres used was to make a slit in a bulky scarf. Adjusting his camera to the best general setting possible, he would hide the camera in the scarf and secretly take random pictures.[7] In this way he recorded history and was a witness with proof of what he saw.

Veres went beyond the risk of taking pictures and at times directly saved lives. Once when he had been called by Wallenberg to the Józsefváros Railway Station, he seized an opportunity while the guards were otherwise occupied and slipped open a bolt on one side of the train. Hundreds of people ran for their lives.[8]

At the end of his time in Budapest, Wallenberg went to meet the Russians on that fateful day in January of 1945. Two days before he left, he asked Veres to go with him. To Wallenberg the meeting was to be a joining of allies where he and the Russians could plan such things as how to restore Jewish property to the rightful owners and how to normalize life once again in Hungary.

But Veres's parents had disappeared, and the younger Veres explained that he had to stay and try to find them. As it turned out, the older couple had been killed by the Arrow Cross and thrown into the Danube. But in that final tragedy of their lives, Berta and Paul Veres had actually saved their son's life, who, because he was looking for his parents, did not join Wallenberg.[9]

The approximately seven hundred provisional passports Per Anger issued in 1944 (eventually with the permission of the foreign office) went to many heads of companies and leading businessmen. These people became the nucleus for Wallenberg's effective rescue work, and their expertise was vital, since it could be utilized immediately without requiring further training. Hugo Wohl, the first man so saved, became second only to Wallenberg in organizing the rescues and is another unsung hero of the Holocaust. Furthermore, Wohl's daughter Edit and her husband, Lars Ernster, worked for Wallenberg. Edit went on to become a concert violinist, while Lars became a well-respected biochemist, but in Budapest Edit worked on the switchboard and Lars performed clerical duties.[10]

One of the first topics of discussion between Anger and Wallenberg had focused on the provisional passes and the visa certificates that the legation had been issuing. Anger showed them to Wallenberg and explained how he had used them to save some key people in the Jewish community. Wallenberg had some creative thoughts relating to the passes themselves: Add the Swedish colors, decorate them with the three Swedish crowns, and include each person's photograph along with official signatures. Wallenberg had a keen understanding of the German mind, and he knew that passes that looked as official as possible would carry more weight with the Germans. In this way Anger's provisional pass became a protective pass known as the *Schutzpass,* the "paper of life and death," according to one survivor.

The same survivor tells a wonderful story that illustrates the importance of that piece of paper. A nine-month-old baby was learning to say his first words. *Putspass* kept coming out of his lips. *Putspass?* No one could figure out what this was. Then one day he said it a little more clearly, and they knew that *Schutzpass,* not *Mama,* had become this baby's first word. Nor was this surprising. Everyone fully realized that to be deported to a concentration camp meant certain death. *Schutzpass* was every Hungarian Jew's most important word. Still the survivor's mother also gave her children small white pills to keep in their pockets—pills of death, just in case they should somehow be taken in spite of the "paper of life and death."[11]

On a lighter side, after an interview I had with Per and Elena Anger at the home of the Los Angeles consul general emeritus Walter Danielson and his charming wife, Beryl, Per looked up over the fireplace at the Swedish coat of arms with its three crowns. He chuckled and said: "You know, when we printed those *Schutzpasses* we never even knew that we had the crowns upside down!" I looked up quickly at the mantelpiece, and until I went back home and looked carefully at the *Schutzpass* I had, I still wouldn't have noticed the mistake. Yet the bearers of that pass from the Swedish legation were often given life, for the Germans respected such ornate and official papers.

The Swedish diplomats who protected the Jews did not even have an embassy in the city; it was only a legation. Today foreign countries establish an embassy in the capital of a country, while consulates are placed in other smaller cities. The ambassador is established in the embassy, while the consulates have consul generals, all answering back to the embassy and ambassador.

But things were different in the 1940s. According to Per Anger:

> Embassies did not exist at that time, except for the big powers. Before the Second World War a country like the United States, for example, would have an embassy in London. . . . But all the other countries had what we called "legations," where the head was not called an "ambassador" but an "envoy" or "minister." . . . After the war, when Norway and Denmark joined NATO, they raised their legations to embassies. . . . The idea spread, *Why should you maintain a legation when other countries had embassies?* . . . You do not have the same rank if you are a legation. So Sweden also raised all legations to the status of embassy, and all the "ministers" or "envoys" had their titles changed to "ambassador." Thus Swedish embassies are quite modern, except in the 1600s or 1700s, when Sweden was a great power with many embassies.[12]

Anger went on to explain that even in small details, like priority in seating arrangements, it can matter a great deal whether or not you have the title of an *embassy* or a *legation*.

According to Anger, when under economic pressures a country shuts down some of its consulates, it is not uncommon for them to keep some of the consulates open by the use of honorary consul generals. Those so appointed have a knowledge and interest in Sweden but are not career diplomats. They are not salaried, but they do receive expense money. Most honorary consul generals are grateful for what they have received from their background in Sweden, which has helped them to succeed in their new country, and so there is a genuine desire to give something back. They are proud of being Swedes and desire to promote Sweden as a nation.[13]

During the early forties, the Swedish legation was very small. The foundation for the rescue of the Jews had started with a handful of diplomats. Minister Carl Ivan Danielsson was a career diplomat, as was the much younger Per Anger. Denes von Mezey, the consular officer, was the only Hungarian in the legation. He worked tirelessly and was rewarded at the end with Swedish citizenship; later he was employed by the Swedish foreign office. Waldemar Langlet was the Swedish academic and Red Cross representative, while Birgit Brulin and Margareta Bauer were the typists.

The tension of war added stress to the legation's atmosphere. Papers to be signed were brought at all hours of the night, and visitors were frequent. The building that housed the legation was not huge. The ground floor basically consisted of offices: a waiting area; a room for von Mezey and the two typists; a chancellery, with one room for Second Secretary Per Anger; and a small room used for deciphering the large numbers of telegrams from Stockholm or for use as an extra conference room.

The second floor of the legation held residential quarters and the minister's study. There was also a music room with a grand piano, which, when time allowed, Minister Danielsson played as a brief respite from the tension around him.

The legation's top floor consisted of the minister's bedroom, guest rooms, a study for the military attaché, and the servants' quarters. In addition, the two female typists lived in one of the houses next door. Their cheerful housekeeping and culinary skills helped lighten the atmosphere of what was otherwise hard work and tense times.[14]

As the amount of work increased in the efforts to rescue Jews, both Jews, who knew that their property would be confiscated by the Nazis and/or the Arrow Cross, and wealthy Hungarians, who would be the target of the oncoming Russian troops, offered property and goods (such as typewriters) to the Swedes for safekeeping. They all knew that this way their chances of recovering their property were higher. They asked only that their property be taken care of. No receipts were given, just trust. In a short period of time, this enabled the Swedish legation to obtain the additional space and supplies they needed for a task that was growing at a rate they normally could not accommodate.[15]

Berg describes Per Anger as the one who buffered much of the stress on the overworked Danielsson. Above all, he portrays Anger as a "loyal and cheerful friend, whose everlasting good humor was a valuable help to us all." According to Berg, no matter how pressured the day, Anger would "shake off the weariness and worries and get us all into a light . . . mood."[16]

Those who have personally known Anger can appreciate that he is a man who has a cup-half-full rather than a cup-half-empty approach to life. When he is disappointed or discouraged, he deals with it and goes on. The years have not diminished this quality, one that was a great boost to the morale of the Swedish legation in 1944–45, as normal life crumbled, business as usual disappeared, and the stakes were literally life and death.

To this diplomatic community and political scene Anger had brought his new bride. The war was escalating and moving relentlessly toward Budapest. For the Jews of Budapest, sanctions that restricted their movements and businesses had increased throughout the first years of the war, and the latent anti-Semitism was intensified under Nazi pressure from outside the country. Yet the organized killing of Jews was held back until the actual invasion of the Nazis in 1944.

For Per and Elena those early, relatively peaceful days in Budapest were precious and short. But Anger has always been a strong believer in doing all you can to make life normal during abnormal conditions. This mind-set held him in good stead throughout his life, both as a companion and as a diplomat. In turn Elena was the perfect wife for a diplomat. Attractive and charming, she also had her own life as an artist.

The peace of Budapest was shattered, however, when the Nazis invaded in March 1944, after Hitler learned that the Hungarians were engaged in talks with the British government. On March 16, the German minister had informed Admiral Miklós Horthy, Hungary's regent, that he must visit the German chancellor. During their meeting Hitler told Horthy that he knew of this attempt to negotiate a separate peace with the United Nations. As a result, Hitler announced, he would occupy Hungary.[17] Soon after, Adolf Eichmann, the man who would become Wallenberg and Anger's major opposition in the battle of wits, came to Budapest. The Jews of Hungary were now in great danger.

The Angers' first child, Birgitta, was born in April, early in the Nazi occupation. Any peacefulness that had lingered in the great city was fast disappearing. On the morning of the day of Birgitta's birth, Elena complained of some pain but felt that there was no hurry. Per took her to the hospital, however, which was at the edge of Budapest, and then went back to do some work at the legation.

Suddenly the alert sounded. During this time one was forbidden to move around town. It also meant that in a few minutes there would be Allied bombing in the city, which had now been taken over by Hitler. The Americans and the British would be flying over, and their planes would not be able to discern a neutral Swedish diplomat from a Nazi soldier.

The bombs were aimed at the big factories along the Danube, but they could miss their target. Furthermore, it was quite possible that at any moment, due to the destruction of roads and bridges, Per could be cut off from access to the hospital. So off he went in his car to the hospital, curfew or no curfew.

After reaching the hospital, Per settled down to reading a newspaper. A nurse came out to announce the birth of a child, and Per turned to see to whom she was talking before he realized that it was *his* baby!

Then came the bombing! The babies in their small beds were hurriedly put into a long, movable carriage, which was put into an elevator. After the babies were brought to the shelter, the parents joined them. They all stayed there for a couple of days.

During that time the Angers encountered a Lutheran pastor, Wolf Ordas, who had studied under a Swedish archbishop and thus knew the Swedish language. Together they planned the christening. It was typical of the Angers to take an uncomfortable and even dangerous situation and use it to plan something for normal life. Later the pastor performed the christening ceremony with all of the diplomatic corps present. Minister Carl Ivan Danielsson was named the godfather. Following tradition, Birgitta's parents even found a bottle of champagne to save for the celebration of her eighteenth birthday.[18]

Life did go on. A baby was born, and tradition was not forgotten, be it as important as the christening of a baby or as minor as keeping a bottle of champagne for eighteen years. As Anger states: "Sometimes you were able to forget about the situation and then concentrate on just those happy moments."[19] Indeed, holding on to some semblance of normalcy was the only way to survive during the nightmare that lay ahead for the Swedes and for the Jews of Budapest.

This 1995 photograph shows Wallenberg's headquarters, which were in the second building from the left. This relatively unchanged building is on the Pest side of Budapest. *(Photographer: Andrew D. Gee. Used by permission.)*

Raoul Wallenberg, seated, with his Jewish co-workers in Budapest in November 1944. Left to right: Dannonbergt; Hugo Wohl, head of the department; Klein; Forgacs; Paul Hegedus; Tibor Sandor; Dr. Otto Fleishmann. *(Photographer: Thomas Veres. Courtesy of the United States Holocaust Memorial Museum.)*

venskt provisoriskt pass.

A provisional passport issued by Anger in April 1944. Officially, these could be issued only to Swedish citizens, but Anger broke this rule to save Hugo Wohl and then other non-Swedes who had close connections in Sweden. Those who were given such a passport were treated as Swedish citizens and were relieved of the obligation to wear the Jewish star. Ultimately, this action was approved by the Swedish government. *(Courtesy of Per Anger family.)*

Provisional passports could only be issued limitedly, since they were intended for people who were actually Swedish citizens. Therefore, a certificate was issued by Per Anger for those Jews who had applied for Swedish citizenship through Swedish relatives in Sweden. This document was the forerunner of the Schutzpass. *(Courtesy of Per Anger family.)*

SCHUTZ-PASS

Nr. 0590

Name: Éva Balog
Név:

Wohnort: Budapest
Lakás:

Geburtsdatum: 15. Oktober 1910.
Születési ideje:

Geburtsort: Budapest
Születési helye:

Körperlänge: 169 cm.
Magasság:

Haarfarbe: braun Augenfarbe: grau
Hajszín: Szemszín:

Unterschrift:
Aláírás:

SCHWEDEN ♛ SVÉDORSZÁG
♛ ✦ ♛

Die Kgl. Schwedische Gesandtschaft in Budapest bestätigt, dass der Obengenannte im Rahmen der — von dem Kgl. Schwedischen Aussenministerium autorisierten — Repatriierung nach Schweden reisen wird. Der Betreffende ist auch in einen Kollektivpass eingetragen.

Bis Abreise steht der Obengenannte und seine Wohnung unter dem Schutz der Kgl. Schwedischen Gesandtschaft in Budapest.

Gültigkeit: erlischt 14 Tage nach Einreise nach Schweden.

A budapesti Svéd Kir. Követség igazolja, hogy fentnevezett — a Svéd Kir. Külügyminisztérium által jóváhagyott — repatriálás keretében Svédországba utazik.

Nevezett a kollektív útlevélben is szerepel.

Elutazásig fentnevezett és lakása a budapesti Svéd Kir. Követség oltalma alatt áll.

Érvényét veszti a Svédországba való megérkezéstől számított tizennegyedik napon.

Reiseberechtigung nur gemeinsam mit dem Kollektivpass. Einreisewisum wird nur in dem Kollektivpass eingetragen.

Budapest, den 19. August *1944*

KÖNIGLICH SCHWEDISCHE GESANDTSCHAFT
SVÉD KIRÁLYI KÖVETSÉG

Kgl. Schwedischer Gesandte

A Schutzpass, often called "the paper of life and death," guaranteed the protection of the Swedish government. The Shutzpass evolved from the previous passes granted by Per Anger, but was also the result of the unique genius of Raoul Wallenberg, in that it was more elaborate and official-looking, a difference that made it more believable to the Germans. *(Courtesy of the Simon Wiesenthal Center Beit HaShoah Museum of Tolerance Library/Archives, Los Angeles, California.)*

The first Jews seeking
help outside of the
Swedish legation in
March 1944.
*(Photographer:
Thomas Veres.
Courtesy of the United
States Holocaust
Memorial Museum.)*

Józsefváros Railway Station in Budapest, which was the location of many
rescues. This station was not used for passengers, but for freight. The station
was built in 1867, but even today still looks like it did in the 1940s.
(Photographer: Richard B. Baltzell. Used by permission.)

Liberation of laborers under Swedish protection from deportation at the Józsefváros Railway Station in Budapest. Wallenberg is thought to be the man in the black hat and coat in the center in the background. Young Tom Veres took many of these pictures secretly through a slit in his scarf. (*Photographer: Thomas Veres. Courtesy of the United States Holocaust Memorial Museum.*)

Jews drafted to clear rubble after the bombings of Budapest. (*Photographer: Elena Anger. Courtesy of Per Anger family.*)

Arrow Cross (Nyilas) outside the Royal Swedish Legation in January 1945. (*Courtesy of Per Anger family.*)

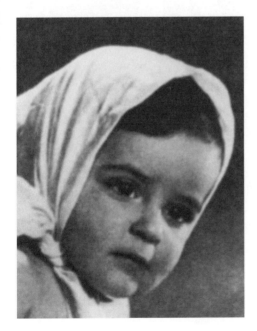

Baby born in Wallenberg's flat (apartment) because her Jewish mother, who worked for Wallenberg, could not get help in a hospital. Wallenberg became her godfather. Many years later, Anger met the goddaughter in Canada. (*Courtesy of Per Anger family.*)

69

A Jewish family moving with their belongings to the Budapest ghetto, April 1944. *(Photographer: Elena Anger. Courtesy of Per Anger family.)*

4

$$\equiv\equiv\equiv\equiv\equiv\equiv\equiv\equiv\equiv\equiv\equiv\equiv$$

Rescuer

A young girl and her mother waited in their home in the Budapest ghetto. Outside they heard the Nyila gangs rounding up Jews who were between the ages of fourteen and sixty-five.[1] *When will our turn come?* the two wondered.

In October 1944, the war in Europe was winding down, and Hitler was losing. Yet in Hungary it seemed as if the war against the Jews was just beginning. For the child, normal expectations like school, best friends, new clothes, and meeting a boy seemed distant and unimportant. Staying alive was the issue at hand.

Then early one October morning, the child and her mother were given twenty minutes to pack and get out. What do you do in twenty minutes to pack up a lifetime? Once outside, they joined others in a march. Their first destination was a brick factory. By this time there were several thousand people marching. Those who walked too slowly were shot. The child and her mother made sure that they walked as quickly as possible.

The brick factory was dark. There were holes in the floor that could not be seen, and those unfortunate people who fell in the holes were trampled over by the Nazi soldiers and the crowds of Jews who were prodded on at gunpoint. Once the factory was filled up with all the people, there was barely room for them to sit. The absence of food, water, medical supplies, or toilets only added to the building's bleakness and their souls' desolation. The armed Nazis walked around stepping on people, cursing, mindlessly abusing, and even shooting.

Morning took a long time coming. But when the day dawned, the waiting continued. The trains had been stopped, so by now most people in the brick factory knew the next stage of their journey was to be a ninety-mile march toward the Austrian border.

Suddenly, at one end of the factory people dressed in civilian clothes seemed to appear out of nowhere. Flashlight beams penetrated the darkness, and a voice sounded over a loudspeaker. One man commanded the situation— a man whose name, *Raoul Wallenberg*, had become a symbol of hope.

The man began to talk to a group of hopeless people who could barely comprehend his presence, much less absorb his words. "I have demanded that each of you who has a *Schutzpass* must be allowed to return to Budapest," he said. Furthermore, still speaking in the dark illuminated only by flashlights, he explained to the crowd that he would send medical help and volunteer doctors and nurses to them, and that toilet facilities would be provided. When he left, the captives felt a renewed sense of dignity and a tiny glimmer of hope.

The next morning the nurses and doctors arrived. Some medical supplies were given out, and wounds and illnesses were treated as well as was possible under those primitive conditions. The people who had been beaten down in their spirits, and some in their bodies, felt some of their sense of worth was restored.

According to one of the witnesses, you could hear from all over the room: *"Shema Yisrael, Adonai eloheinu, Adonai ehad."*[2] These lines, which were also often heard on the lips of those going to the gas chambers of the concentration camps, came from a prayer that practicing Jews say twice a day. The words come from the Bible, "Hear, O Israel: The LORD our God, the LORD is one" (Deut. 6:4 NIV). They reflect a personal acceptance of faith in God in any circumstances and acceptance of God's sovereignty in the world.

For some the words may have been a preparation for death. For others they may have expressed the beginning of hope. For all of the captives the time passed slowly. Night came and went. There was still no water or food, but there was a glimmer of encouragement.

At sunrise, preparations were made to start the long march to Austria. Some captives were too ill to walk. Most had improper shoes and clothing for such a challenge. Nevertheless the march would go on, and those who could not make it would be shot or simply left to die. It was cheaper that way.

Then, once again, Wallenberg appeared. This time he came with trucks. Under Wallenberg's watchful eye, the Nazi soldiers told the people to show their *Schutzpasses.* The child and her mother were among the lucky ones who had passes, so they were among the few hundred saved that day.

Stunned, as if coming out of a nightmare, the child and her mother joined those who had been saved and were now heading back to Budapest, this time in a truck rather than on foot. They had been saved by a man who at any time could have been shot and thrown in the Danube for his deeds of humanitarianism.

Others could not be saved, not even by Wallenberg. Hopelessly, thousands of them continued on their way to ultimate death in the extermination camp that was to be their final destination.[3]

For the Germans, the death march was the act of ultimate cruelty and desperation as they began to lose power.

> It was Eichmann who had decided that if the trains could no longer be spared to transport the Jews to their deaths, then they should walk. Early in November he started the death marches. . . . The distance had to be covered on foot without any real food or shelter along the way. For at least 10,000 people, who died of exhaustion or hunger or thirst, the march itself accomplished the job Eichmann was impatient to get on with.
>
> The marches started whenever the Nazis could round up enough Jews to start them walking: on street corners, in shops, in their own homes. No Jew was completely safe from the fatal convoy. Soon the roadside from Budapest to Hegyashalom was one long graveyard. Those who stumbled and fell were generally finished off with a single bullet. Others used the overnight rest in village squares or in open fields to end their own lives: bodies were often found hanging limply from the trees the next morning. . . . The endless columns snaked through the countryside, covering twenty miles a day.[4]

But remaining in Budapest was no guarantee of safety for the Jews.

> Eichmann . . . had a proprietary feeling about Budapest. He had spent more time there than any other high-ranking Nazi. He felt he had earned the right to dispose of its Jews as he saw fit. . . .
>
> Eichmann relied on the highly successful model of the Warsaw ghetto in drawing up his plans for Budapest's. Six-foot-high planks were thrown up by Arrow Cross toughs, blocking off the streets that framed the three synagogues of the capital, the former Jewish quarter. And

12,000 Christians were moved out to make way for 63,000 Jews.

Eichmann's captives could not leave to obtain medicine or to take care of any other emergency. They were completely dependent on their guards to bring them food, which often meant long days without the necessities of life.[5]

Shortly before the Soviet liberation, Wallenberg complained to the Germans of the conditions in the walled ghetto:

Some 53,000 persons inhabit the Budapest Ghetto. . . . Of these, several thousand suffer from under-nourishment and are lying in the tenement houses used as hospitals. Most of these people have no mattresses and many lack even blankets. The Ghetto is not heated. Originally, the area . . . was inhabited by 15,000 people, and under these conditions the Jews are living at a scale worse than any Hungarian refugee. Naturally, they have no soap and very little water and but a few candles. As it is impossible to accommodate the whole of the population in the air-raid shelters during the attacks, the death rate . . . is higher than anywhere else in the capital.

On paper, the authorities of the capital have made a food allotment of 900 calories per head a day. . . . The lowest ration in prisons amounts to 1,500 a day.[6]

From July 9, 1944, to January 17, 1945, Wallenberg carried out his work for the Swedish legation. In the end, he was captured by the Russian "liberators" and left in the Russian prison system until this day. Simon Wiesenthal, who has worked relentlessly in the search for Wallenberg, sums up best the viewpoint of many: "Raoul Wallenberg is alive as long as the Russians don't give us believable information about his death."[7]

By the time of his capture, Wallenberg had saved 100,000 of the Jews of Budapest from death at the hands of the Nazis. These figures are sometimes disputed, and some put the figure at between 20,000 and 30,000, but the explanation is a simple one. Using protective passes and Swedish safe houses, Wallenberg saved about 30,000 people. However, at the end of the war, as the Russians were entering Budapest, Nazi tanks and guns were stationed outside of the large, closed ghetto that housed at that time about 70,000 Jews. Orders had been given to blow up the ghetto before the Russians could rescue the inhabitants. When Wallenberg heard of this, he sent a message to the general who was responsible for this action. By threatening him with war crime trials after the war and promising to testify for him if he would cooperate, Wallenberg convinced the general to rescind the order to destroy the ghetto. In that way he saved another 70,000 Jews.

The ghetto was opened on January 16, 1945. Wallenberg was taken by the Russians one day later. A witness claims that on the morning of the seventeenth, while he was standing at the entrance to a hospital, he saw Wallenberg, accompanied by two men he did not recognize. There was a short conversation between the witness and Wallenberg, during which time this witness told Wallenberg some things that had been happening concerning the hospital. As they were walking and conversing together, suddenly Wallenberg slipped on the icy pavement. As he started to get up he happened to see three very old men, still wearing the yellow star. With tears in his eyes and in some pain from his fall, he turned to this witness and said: "I am glad that my mission has not been entirely unsuccessful."[8]

The question with Raoul Wallenberg is always *why*? Why did he, a member of the wealthy Wallenberg banking family, go to Budapest and risk his life? Why did the Russians take him captive? Why didn't the world, and especially the Swedish government, immediately demand his release? We may not be able to answer all the questions, but we must make some effort to comprehend them and the man behind them if we are to understand the interaction between this great man and another great man, Per Anger.

Raoul Wallenberg was born in Sweden on August 12, 1912. Tragically, his father, Raoul Oscar Wallenberg, a naval officer of only twenty-five years of age, died three months before his son's birth. Raoul's paternal grandfather, Ambassador Gustaf Wallenberg, became the main influence on his childhood years.

When his grandfather died in 1937, Raoul lost a tremendous source of emotional support. Yet throughout his brief life in Sweden, he was surrounded by a loving family. He was always close to his mother, Maj. She had remarried when Raoul was six years old, and Raoul had gained a father and eventually a half brother, Guy, and half sister, Nina. His stepfather, Fredrik von Dardel, tried to take the place of Raoul's dead father, and a great deal of love existed between all the members of the family.

Even as a very small child Raoul possessed a certain sensitivity and precociousness. For example, one day when he was quite young he was found crying in front of his father's picture. When asked the reason for his distress, he replied: "Raoul has no father, I feel sorry for him." When he was a little older, unlike his friends, he showed no fear of thunderstorms. Asked why, he replied: "This is God's fireworks, different from that of men."[9]

Language studies and a knowledge of other countries were emphasized by his grandfather. At an early age Raoul took study trips to different countries, where he mastered German, French, and English and developed a feel for international affairs. All of this would greatly help him when he went to Budapest to save Jews. At school he had no interest in boyish pranks or team sports, yet he gained the respect of his fellow classmates by his broad and varied knowledge of subjects way beyond his age.

Much of this knowledge he had gained on his own. For example, he had read in their entirety the thirty-five volumes of Sweden's most complete encyclopedia. In addition to his pursuit of knowledge regarding people and the times in which they lived, he also enjoyed music and had a very fine singing voice. Because of that talent, he sang in the church choir, and in later years Raoul invited a favorite aunt to go with him to hear *St. Matthew's Passion* at the Stockholm Cathedral each year.

The Bible, too, was a book he often read, and he had a thorough knowledge of its teachings. An aunt of Raoul's remembers a visit he made as an adult to her home in Mexico. Raoul became ill, and "during his fever Raoul frequently spoke in Biblical similes. It is my conviction," continued the aunt, "that in his own way and in his deepest self, he was quite religious. This is the reason why he always made fun of artificial trimmings and formalities in churches."[10]

After graduation from what would be the Swedish equivalent of high school, it was customary for students to take a month off and do nothing. But Raoul was not good at doing nothing, so he immediately joined the world-famous Stockholm Enskilda Bank as a short-term volunteer. The Wallenberg family were the major shareholders in this bank. But a few years later, in a 1937 letter from Haifa, Raoul wrote to his grandfather:

> You mustn't lose sight of one thing, and that is that I may not be particularly suited for banking at all. Do you think, for example, that you would have thought me capable of assuming your mantle in this area if I were not your grand-

son? . . . To tell you the truth, I don't find myself very bankerish: the director of a bank should be judgelike and calm and cold and cynical. . . . My temperament is better suited to some positive line of work than to sitting around saying no.[11]

After his brief experience in the bank, Raoul performed his required 250 days service in the military. Then, at nineteen, he entered the University of Michigan in the United States, where he studied architecture. The experience left him very enthusiastic about American life.

After leaving the United States, Raoul continued his travels. By the time he went to Haifa, not only were his ideas set regarding banking as a career, but he had also come to other conclusions that would determine the course of the rest of his life: He had begun to understand the plight of the Jewish race. In a letter to his grandfather written from Haifa in 1936, Raoul expressed a deep positive feeling for the Jews, which existed apart from the sense of urgency that would come later when Hitler's killing machines started functioning. Raoul wrote:

To them [the Jews], Palestine is much more than a mere refuge; it is the promised land, the land designated for them by God. It will take an enormous effort to make the country suitable for farming, for there is very little water and much too much stone. Before they arrived there were only about 800,000 Arabs, if that many, and they would like to reach a Jewish population of 4,000,000. When a foreigner asks how the country will feed that many, they reply with a beautiful fable. Palestine, they say, is like the skin of a deer. When the skin is removed from the animal, it shrinks, and you wonder how it could ever have covered the animal. It is the same with Palestine: so long as Palestine contains a Jewish population, it drips with milk and honey and can support a large population; when there are no longer any Jews, it shrinks in value, unable to support even a small Arab population and its minuscule demands.[12]

According to Anger, at this time Wallenberg made up his mind to help the Jews. In Haifa he saw Jews coming for refuge. He heard stories of persecution. Anger feels Wallenberg said to himself: *Oh, my God, I have to do something here. I have to do something.*[13] Visiting Haifa was one of those life experiences that helped to prepare him for his future mission.

Haifa was a catapult into the future when Wallenberg would be asked to go to Budapest and save Jews. It provided a point of readiness that would lead to an affirmative answer when the challenge directly confronted him. But the real answer as to why he responded so vigorously to the challenge to save Jews lies in the inner personality and character of Raoul Wallenberg. In short, who was Raoul Wallenberg?

To those who know the Wallenberg story at all, it seems strange to say that he called himself a *Hassenfuss*—a "timid rabbit." Particularly during his time in Budapest, he is sometimes portrayed as a fearless man who took no thought for safety. In reality, Raoul was very aware of the dangers that surrounded him, but his focus was on the task for which he had come—to save the Jews. Wallenberg loved life greatly, but he had an ability to show compassion in the face of fear that makes him far more heroic than he would have been if he had had a desire for death or a stupid inability to see the danger.

As they shared the war's dangers, Per Anger became Wallenberg's good friend. The two Swedish diplomats grew close in the midst of their hectic activities in which Per played a large role in maintaining a diplomatic front, while Raoul was usually the one saving Jewish lives. Per describes Wallenberg as a compassionate man who always wanted to help people who were in need. It was a pattern that had started long before the war began.

When Anger talked to Wallenberg's fellow students at the University of Michigan, they told him many stories of how Wallenberg always went out of his way to help people.

One of Wallenberg's friends from way back, according to Anger, was a Jewish boy whom he knew in Switzerland. Raoul and this boy were students together. Because of his small stature and delicate looks, the Jewish student appeared unable to defend himself. As a result, he became the brunt of teasing and general bad treatment by other students. At the beginning of their relationship, Raoul came up to the boy and said: "Don't be afraid. I'm going to defend you against these other, bigger boys here." While other people become heroes because they are confronted head-on with the necessity to save a life or help someone, Anger explained, Wallenberg did it almost as a natural act of living. He was just that kind of person.[14]

Compassion and courage intermingled in Wallenberg's acts in Budapest, as an incident that occurred in November 1944 illustrates most aptly. A bunker was set up to hide over twenty children who would otherwise have been killed by the Nazis because they were Jewish. However, the children were discovered, and some Arrow Cross thugs lined them up to be executed. As the Nazis stood with their guns, Wallenberg appeared, as he did so often, seemingly out of nowhere. He stood between the children and the soldiers' guns, screaming: "You will have to kill me if you kill these children." The soldiers backed off, and the children were saved.[15]

In Wallenberg compassion and courage joined in an almost seamless line. They merged with a grace that almost seemed to make the events too good to be true, but

100,000 lives are witness to the fact that these events represented life at its most real level.

Without his resourcefulness, however, Wallenberg would never have survived his bravery. He could think on his feet, act with wisdom in a split second, and make something work in ways no one else thought of. According to Anger, Wallenberg's ability to negotiate was one of his strongest qualities and may have achieved more than any other technique he employed.

The application of his intellect to practical needs gave Wallenberg a powerful tool in helping people. As a young man in the military, for example, in a training exercise his troops were commanded to go over a river. The only problem was that all the bridges had been blown up. A nearby sign read: "Bridge Blown Up." Instead of quitting, Wallenberg went down to the river to a man who was sitting in a large boat. "How much would it cost to bring the whole troop over?" he asked. After paying the man, Wallenberg returned to his captain and said: "Sir, everything is arranged. I have a boat there for all of us to go over."

Another time Wallenberg was supposed to be with his platoon at the palace for inspection. When the captain came to inspect the troops and asked for Raoul, his friends replied: "He's down at the harbor. He's training his soldiers to defend the port." It made sense, at least to Wallenberg. He was by this time a businessman, and his firm stored products at the harbor. So he trained the troops to defend that storage. He was only a sergeant, but that didn't matter. He felt the need to be resourceful, to think, to figure out solutions on his own.[16]

Later, in Budapest, such personal training probably saved many lives. Anger tells of a time at the Austrian border when students were just about to be handed over to Eichmann. Only two had any kind of protective passport. In the brusque, self-assured manner he used so often with the Nazis, Wallenberg barked out: "You must know that all your passports have been confiscated by the authorities. All of you who have had a passport that was taken should come forward now." Not surprisingly, most of them stepped away from the border and went back to Budapest with Wallenberg.[17]

Incidents such as this repeated themselves over and over again in those closing months of the war. The miracle was that no one ever really stopped Wallenberg. They threatened to shoot him, but they didn't. Once Eichmann tried to kill him, but he failed. Only at the end did the Russians—the Allies, not the Axis—succeed in taking Wallenberg captive. His friends, not his enemies, were his captors.

Part of the strength of Wallenberg's resourcefulness lay in his desire to grow, his need to constantly improve upon what he did, even when those actions had been successful. When he was still a student in the United States, Raoul was hitchhiking on his way home from a visit to Chicago and was picked up by four men. Certain aspects of their demeanor made him suspicious, but it was not until they turned off onto an obscure country lane that he became truly alarmed. The four ruffians stopped and got out of the car. Brandishing a gun, they ordered Raoul out of the car and demanded his money. Wallenberg gave them the money he had in his breast pocket and told them that there was more in the suitcase. The suitcase also contained a key to his safety deposit box, but Raoul managed to keep the key by bluffing about its sentimental nature. Determined that he should get something back for what had been taken from him, Raoul convinced them to drive him back to school. As they were driving to their destination, Raoul's calm attitude made them frightened and suspicious, and the thugs abruptly threw Raoul and, fortunately, his luggage out of the car.

In a letter to his grandfather, where he describes the incident in detail, Raoul concludes: "This will not make me give up hitchhiking. I'll just carry less money on me, and try to become more devious."[18] In another version written to his mother, he says: "I will note this experience and do it better in the future."[19]

One other essential character ingredient made Wallenberg successful in his efforts to save the Jews: the determination never to give up. He had developed perseverance all through his life. Raoul had an almost contemptuous attitude toward sports, yet he trained his body to the point where even the most devoted sportsman had difficulty competing with him. During a hunt, Raoul and several others decided to cross a lake covered in snow. His companions gave up after one or two kilometers. Raoul, on the other hand, went the full five kilometers and reached the other shore.[20]

In his last experience with Per Anger in Budapest, just before he was captured and imprisoned by the Russians, Wallenberg showed his determination to persevere to the end. Wallenberg had arranged a meeting with the Russians; his goal was to help the Jews recover their property after the war and in general to help the transition from war to peace. Anger sensed the danger in the meeting and begged him to stay in Buda and not go back to Pest. Recounted Anger: "The last time I saw Wallenberg was the 10th of January 1945. He paid me a brief visit and I remember how I pleaded insistently with him to suspend his operation and stay with us on the Buda side." The Hungarian Nazis were looking for him, bombs were falling, and when they got into a car to drive, dead bodies, horses, toppled trees, and shattered buildings constantly blocked their way. Anger asked, "Aren't you frightened?"

"Sure, it gets a little scary, sometimes," Wallenberg said, "but for me there's no choice. I've taken on this assignment and I'd never be able to go back to Stockholm without knowing inside myself I'd done all a man could do to save as many Jews as possible."[21]

In an ironic twist of fate, the young boy from Switzerland whom Wallenberg had promised to protect was the last person to see him before he was taken by the Russians. As a man he had kept up his contact with Wallenberg. Now he shared that last fateful ride to meet with the Russians. Langfelder, Wallenberg's faithful chauffeur, commented that Buda would soon be taken over by the Russians. The young Jewish man became very concerned about his parents, who were hiding in Buda, and he decided that he should leave Wallenberg and go back to find them.

Wallenberg understood and by that understanding once again protected his friend, this time without knowing it. They parted with warmth, and the car disappeared into the unknown. The only other witness was the faithful Langfelder who, along with Wallenberg, was never directly heard from again.[22]

Author Jeno Levai has presented Wallenberg as representing the "'watchful eyes of the world'. He was the ever present 'judge', demanding an explanation."[23] Neither the German Nazis nor the Arrow Cross could trick him. The war was winding down. The Allies were winning, and their bombs could be seen and felt all over the city. The Nazis feared war crime trials, and as long as Wallenberg was watching them, their behavior was inhibited. It was not quite as easy to feel free to persecute the helpless while there was someone whose presence made you accountable.

Raoul Wallenberg was the right man, in the right place, at the right time. Due to the political structure of Hungary and its relationship to the Reich during World War II, what Wallenberg did in Budapest worked, while it might not have worked anywhere else. We need not ask, "Why weren't there more Raoul Wallenbergs?" Raoul Wallenberg was right where he was needed most and could be used best.

The real question we need to ask is, "How many of the rest of us are willing to be accountable for and to each other where we live?"

One Man's Imprint for Evil

or Paul it was a normal day of work at the factory in Budapest where he was an electrical engineer. Even the cold weather was not unusual for that time of year.

Suddenly that normal day became the most abnormal one of his life, and the year 1944 would never be forgotten. Soldiers broke into the work routine and took away any workers who were Jews. Paul was one of those who was marched away in a group, joining with people taken from other factories. Their destination? Railroad cattle cars packed above their capacity with about eighty per car. Their crime? They were Jews!

To Paul it seemed that at least one thousand people, young and old, were taken on that march from the factory to the railroad. The soldiers, using the bayonets attached to their rifles, prodded their captives on to their destination. As the cars were filled up, other SS soldiers stood around and watched, arrogant in their highly polished boots, immaculate uniforms, and shining medals.

Then in what were prolonged minutes of horror, a few women appeared unexpectedly. One by one they each wished to say good-bye to a beloved sweetheart, husband, or son. Filling the air with obscene language, the SS officers grabbed the women and shoved them into a cattle car already filled to capacity with men. Their loved ones could only stand by helplessly and watch, for to intervene would have meant immediate death for all involved.

With equal suddenness a new arrival appeared on the scene. He was a young civilian dressed unobtrusively in a trench coat. A whisper circulated among the Jews who still stood waiting: "Wallenberg is here! Wallenberg is here!" Paul thought Raoul Wallenberg looked frail. It seemed a miracle, not only that he had come, but that he could possibly do anything against such force.

Paul was one of the last in line, so he had plenty of time to observe. Going over to the towering, well-fed, well-dressed officers, Wallenberg demanded in a calm but authoritative voice that everyone with a *Schutzpass* should be disembarked and taken back to one of the Swedish safe houses. After some heated debate, he won his point. Paul was still a few feet away and could both see and hear with considerable accuracy. According to him, Wallenberg's arguments were cogent and dignified.

At this point a small wooden table was set up with a single chair. Adolf Eichmann, the notorious architect of the Final Solution, seated himself on the chair, thus declaring himself in control. Other SS officers stood behind him. Characteristically, Wallenberg stationed himself at the side of the table, quietly assuming his own position of authority as a member of the Swedish legation. Anyone who had a Swedish document was taken to the queue in the front of the table. Then the SS officers examined each document. Every time an officer decided that the pass was genuine or fake a life hung in the balance. The SS wanted to find as many fake documents as possible, while Wallenberg tried to make each piece of paper save a life. Sometimes out of frustration or for effect—or maybe for a little of each—he would slam his fist down on the table.

Paul was near the end of the line. He had only one small piece of paper, neatly folded four times and treasured safely in the breast pocket of his shirt. It was only a carbon copy of a two-line typewritten form with the date of issue, Paul's name, and the signature of someone with the Swedish legation. It had come to be one of his most precious possessions. He had received this piece of paper upon the recommendation of the Swedish company for which he worked, and it proved only that his application for a visa had been received.

When Paul showed his precious piece of paper to the officer at the table the officer pushed it away with the words "not relevant." Quickly Wallenberg pointed to two small letters on the bottom left-hand corner of the document and exclaimed: "They are my initials." Concluded Paul: "I was saved by one man's determination and compulsion for humanity from deportation, death-camp, torture, starvation, and ultimately, from the gas chamber." As Paul started back to the city, he could hear the train as it began its tragic journey to death.[1]

Adolf Eichmann was born on March 19, 1906, in Solingen, Germany, a town famous for making scissors, knives, and surgical instruments. His father was an accountant, and his mother died when Eichmann was ten years old. His parents had five children, four boys and one girl, of whom Eichmann was the eldest. Eichmann never finished either high school or vocational school, a fact that he blamed on his father's economic status, ignoring the fact that his brothers and sister all managed to graduate.

Before he found his niche in the Third Reich, Eichmann's only real success was the five or six years he spent as a salesman for the Vacuum Oil Company, during which

A Quiet Courage

time he lived at home. Meanwhile, in 1932 Adolf Eichmann joined the Nazi Party, the National Socialist Party. In early 1933 he was transferred to Salzburg, where he claims to have lost all interest in his work. This man whose life had so far been a failure, a person who never did read the bible of Nazism, Hitler's *Mein Kampf,* was about to make a career that had as its price tag the lives of six million Jews. Centuries of European anti-Semitism; the more immediate factor in Germany of economic deprivation resulting from the Versailles Treaty; the charismatic charm of another loser in real life, Adolf Hitler, with his disillusionment over his lack of acceptance as an artist: All these combined to form fertile soil in which an otherwise boring failure was to become a notorious world figure.

To relegate Eichmann's success exclusively to the mundane, however, is to underestimate the power of evil in this world. Long before the Holocaust, in 1865 the famous English preacher Charles Haddon Spurgeon said the following almost prophetic words: "No nation has ever yet risen above the character of its so-called gods.... 'A people are never better than their religion,' it has often been said, and in most cases they are rather worse."[2]

According to Hannah Arendt, in her book *Eichmann in Jerusalem,* at the time of his trial Eichmann declared himself to be a *Gottgläubiger,* the Nazi term for those who had renounced Christianity.[3] While the term literally means "believer in God," the Nazis coined the word for their own use. It became jargon for a belief that included denial of the Christian God and a statement that they, the Nazis, had their own gods. Renunciation of Christ as well as of the Old Testament Jehovah was common with the Nazis. A person who belonged to a Christian church could not expect acceptance in the Nazi Party. Furthermore, to rise in the party inevitably required a person to be a *Gottgläubiger.*

The Nazis replaced the Christian God with a god that was called a *Höheren Sinnesträger,* which gave him a place linguistically in the military hierarchy. Furthermore, each of those connected with the Final Solution was officially called a "bearer of secrets," a *Geheimnisträger.*[4] Initiations often involved formal occult rituals. This was especially true of those directly involved with the Final Solution and therefore would have probably included Eichmann. That the Third Reich, and very specifically the focus on the genocide of the Jews, was integrally related to blatant occult connections would seem to be beyond debate.

Thus, while much of the Christian world at large was well aware of Nazism and the atrocities to the Jews and failed to oppose this, Christians were not among the top leaders in the Nazi Party. These men were, at least nominally, the worshipers of the ancient Teutonic gods; they had most certainly renounced the God as well as the heaven of the Judeo-Christian tradition. They did not worship Jehovah of the Old Testament, and they actively denied the Messiah of the New Testament.

The results of his denial of Christianity were reflected in Eichmann's behavior throughout his life. Fellow Nazi Dieter Wisliceny was asked, "Did he [Eichmann] say anything at that time as to the number of Jews that had been killed?" His flippant response was, "Yes, he expressed this in a particularly cynical manner. He said he would leap laughing in the grave because the feeling that he had five million people on his conscience would be for him a source of extraordinary satisfaction."[5]

At his trial in Jerusalem Eichmann refused to take an oath on the Bible. Even at the time of his execution he flaunted God. During the last two hours of his life, when a Protestant pastor offered to read the Bible with him, he turned the offer down because he had no "time to waste." He died declaring once again that he was a *Gottgläubiger*

91

and not a Christian and that he did not believe in life after death.[6]

One is reminded of the words of the psalmist:

> For these men brag of all their evil lusts; they revile God. . . .
>
> These wicked men, so proud and haughty, seem to think that God is dead. They wouldn't think of looking for him! . . .
>
> But the Lord is still in his holy temple; he still rules from heaven. He closely watches everything that happens here on earth. He puts the righteous and the wicked to the test; he hates those loving violence. He will rain down fire and brimstone on the wicked and scorch them with his burning wind.
>
> For God is good, and he loves goodness; the godly shall see his face.
>
> Psalms 10:3–4; 11:4–7 TLB

Much of what the Nazis stood for was also in direct contrast to the beliefs of some of the regular German army, which was composed of many who had no connection with the old pagan gods of the Nazis and who became increasingly disenchanted with both Hitler and Nazism as the war went on and the atrocities increased. One of the heroes of World War II was Count von Stauffenberg, a member of the German army who tried three times to set off a bomb that would kill Hitler. The third time the bomb did go off, but Hitler did not die. Von Stauffenberg was executed the same day.

In his portrayal of von Stauffenberg in his historical novel, Paul West effectively presents the conflict and moral dilemma of a good man faced with seemingly unresolvable evil. According to West, as von Stauffenberg was making the plans for the assassination attempts, he once said to a friend: "I'm a ritual killer. Will I ever be normal again? After something so awful?"

His friend replied: "You will always be you to those of us who know you. What the rest think won't matter."[7]

There was a sense of deep conflict in von Stauffenberg. It was not easy for a good man to kill—not even to kill a Hitler. So in West's portrayal von Stauffenberg sought solace in "Pastor Niemöller's church in St. Anne's: a gesture, inasmuch as Niemöller had been in one concentration camp or another since before the war began. A small service was underway, a tidy fluctuating hum, and I knelt at the back for ten or fifteen minutes, telling my maker that I'd never kill again, I'd never even hate, but on this occasion I would. I wanted holy auspices for an unholy act."[8]

The mass killer, *Gottgläubiger,* and Nazi Adolf Eichmann could kill with joy, while the army officer and Resistance leader Count von Stauffenberg, who had a normal sense of morality, suffered under the strain of his act.

Some time during the confusion of March 1944, Adolf Eichmann arrived in Hungary. His job? Rid Europe of the largest remaining intact group of Jews. He came with a loyal group of assistants, and he set up his office at the luxurious Majestic Hotel.[9] Ultimately he had 150 to 200 people under his immediate command. Over his door a sign was posted: *Judenkommando.* It was perhaps the most feared sign in all of Hungary.

At the time of Eichmann's arrival there were probably close to one million Jews left in Hungary. Many people believed that the war against Hitler had already been won. Yet when Eichmann was asked about the necessity of bothering with this last group of Jews, he clearly answered that the Jews of Hungary must not be left to breed and carry on the Jewish race. When someone argued that the job was futile, that even if the Jews of Europe were destroyed there would be the large group of Jews who remained safe in the United States, he replied that the Jews of America did not trouble him. They would intermarry and in a few generations would cease to exist as Jews. It was the Jews of Europe who would carry on the race. Quite clearly genocide, not just mass murder, was Eichmann's goal. The struggle was over the survival of the Jewish race.

Eichmann and Wallenberg became mortal enemies in this struggle. With Anger, these men became the main players in this final stage of World War II in Hungary.

Though Anger remained in the background and in that sense was Wallenberg's silent partner, he played a crucial role. Wallenberg's ability to act depended upon the work of the neutral Swedish legation.

As second secretary to the Swedish legation, second in command only to Minister Danielsson, it was important for Anger to keep looking neutral, or Wallenberg's work, which was to aggressively save Jews, would have been jeopardized. Wallenberg's only protection was the neutrality of Sweden.

To preserve this neutral front, Anger made sure that he and Eichmann never met. Budapest had a German embassy, which dealt with the neutral embassies, of which the Swedes were one of several. The embassy was the point of Anger's contact, not the Reich. Conversely, Eichmann did not report to the German embassy but directly to Himmler, the head of the SS, who reported to Hitler himself. Therefore, when Wallenberg had his first meeting with Eichmann in midsummer of 1944 at the Arizona nightclub in Budapest, purposely Per Anger was not there.[10]

At that meeting Eichmann and Wallenberg discussed safe houses, negotiations to save Jews, and in general sized up each other. Eichmann's evaluation, according to Simon Wiesenthal, was that Wallenberg was "'soft . . . another decadent diplomat.'"[11] Rarely has one man's evaluation been so far from right. Wallenberg was going to prove his strength to a degree that would defeat Eichmann's final goal. Together Wallenberg and Anger proved deadly foes of the Nazi machine.

While Wallenberg and Anger, as well as other heroic neutrals, were trying to save Jews, Eichmann, under the command of Himmler, set in motion a killing machine that functioned with terrifying speed. Says Arendt: "Eichmann's 'dream' was an incredible nightmare for the Jews: nowhere else were so many people deported and exterminated in such a brief span of time. In less than two months, 147 trains, carrying 434,351 people in sealed freight cars, a hundred persons to a car, left the country, and the gas chambers of Auschwitz were hardly able to cope with the multitude."[12]

According to one source, in the few months Eichmann spent in Hungary, he sent more than 400,000 Jews to their deaths.[13] Another source, which bases its numbers on the Eichmann trial and on a particular conversation with the prosecutor at the trial, places the deportation of Jews from Hungary between May 15 and July 7 at 600,000. Most often, the figures stated, there were four trains a day, each containing a total of 12,000 persons.[14] Many of these were taken to Auschwitz, where they were gassed.

Others died on the infamous death march, when they dropped dead from the exhaustion of a ninety-mile walk, died of disease, or were shot for walking too slowly. Still others were tied together in threes and stood at the edge of the Danube. Then the middle person was shot, which pulled all three into the icy waters of the Danube, where they all died.

Yet in spite of these atrocities, during his capture and trial in Jerusalem the psychiatrists found Eichmann to be psychologically normal; as one psychiatrist put it, more normal than he himself was after talking to Eichmann![15]

Such a finding raises once again the question of *Why?* And once again one concludes that perhaps Eichmann was indeed more evil than mentally ill.

Eichmann's own explanation regarding his behavior is the least complicated of all. Asked about how he could slaughter millions of Jews, Eichmann would give mundane answers like, "I was obeying orders" (a common Nazi response to such a question). During the Eichmann trial, Per Anger was told by the prosecutor that when he had asked Eichmann how he could be a good father, with children who loved him and whom he loved, and a mass murderer at the same time, Eichmann had replied that it was very simple. "That was my job."[16]

Obedience to orders seemed to be blatantly contradicted, however, by the published transcript of the Eichmann trial. Late in the war, SS Chief Himmler wanted to slow Eichmann down in his zeal in killing Jews in order to save himself from postwar trial and execution. By the time this incident occurred, Hitler was losing the war, and war trials were becoming inevitable.

During the trial, Karl Becher, who had been part of the Nazi army, said, "I would like to describe to you a violent outburst. Mr. Himmler received Eichmann for ten minutes while I was there and shouted at him: 'If until now you have murdered the Jews and I now order you to foster Jews, tell me whether you are going to carry out this order of mine or not.'"

Apparently, Himmler received no assurance of obedience to a change of orders. In desperation, Becher felt compelled to further plead his cause with Himmler, hoping that Himmler's rank and power could yet stop Eichmann in his last, frantic effort to annihilate the Jews. Continued Becher: "I begged Himmler, practically on my knees, 'for God's sake, straighten things out again with Eichmann before he leaves your quarters.'"

Once again, Eichmann gave no indication of willingness to comply with Himmler's orders. His silence spoke eloquently. Indeed Himmler concluded the discussion with a gesture that seemed singularly aimed at soothing Eichmann's injured ego. "He was then awarded the Iron Distinguished Service Cross, First Class, with swords, and Eichmann was placated. This is a 'story' I have never told before," concluded Becher.[17] Eichmann went back to killing Jews until he escaped unobtrusively at the end of the war. Eventually he was tracked down in South America.

On May 23, 1960, at his home in Austria, Nazi-hunter Simon Wiesenthal received a cable from Jerusalem. It read: "Congratulations on your excellent work." The event celebrated? The capture of Adolf Eichmann, the architect of Hitler's Final Solution. After studying the cable for a while, Wiesenthal gave it to his teenage daughter with the words: "You never saw your father when you were a baby. You were asleep when I went to work looking for this man and asleep by the time I came home. I don't know how long I will live. I don't know if I will leave you any fortune at all. But this cable is my gift to you. Because through this cable I am now a part of history."[18]

After his capture in 1960, Eichmann explained obsessively the reason why he once slapped a Jew across the face, arguing that he didn't think he had hurt the man and explaining that he had then apologized to him. Yet, in contrast, he faced the killing of five million Jews with indifference. Simon Wiesenthal commented:

> The worst story I can ever tell you about Adolf Eichmann, took place during the time he was in Budapest. In the fall of 1944, a group of high-level SS officers were sitting in the SS casino there. And one of them asked Eichmann how many people had been exterminated already.

97

[Eichmann said: "Over five million."]

Well, because he was among comrades and they all knew it was only a matter of time before they would lose the war, one of them asked whether he was worried about what would happen to him.

Eichmann gave a very astute answer that shows he knew how the world worked: "A hundred dead people is a catastrophe," he said. "Six million dead is a statistic."[19]

Once again, perhaps the lack of psychological explanations makes the issue of the evil of the Third Reich an even greater factor to be reckoned with. It also makes a statement by Hannah Arendt more frighteningly plausible:

Once a specific crime has appeared for the first time, its reappearance is more likely than its initial emergence could ever have been. The particular reasons that speak for the possibility of a repetition of the crimes committed by the Nazis are even more plausible. The frightening coincidence of the modern population explosion with the discovery of technical devices that, through automation, will make large sections of the population "superfluous" even in terms of labor, and that, through nuclear energy, make it possible to deal with this twofold threat by the use of instruments beside which Hitler's gassing installations look like an evil child's fumbling toys, should be enough to make us tremble.[20]

Except for his part in the Final Solution, everything about Eichmann seems mediocre and mundane. Only in the killing of Jews did he become somebody. However, instead of gleefully dancing in his grave with the memory of killing millions of Jews, Eichmann did indeed run to save his life. For years he once again lived a life of mediocrity, this time living in a small house in a run-down neighborhood in Argentina, where he routinely caught a bus to and from work each day at a Mercedes-Benz factory.[21] A little boy was seen playing in the yard, a child who had been born in Argentina and knew nothing about the Eichmann who had terrorized the Jews of Hungary.

That little boy, now grown up, is an archeologist and teacher in Germany. Of his father, Ricardo Eichmann says, "I can't find words to describe the horrible things he did." Indeed, the son seems anything but mediocre. He does not hide who he is, but he also wants to go on. He is not allowing his children to live in ignorance but is teaching them about their past. To his students he says, "If you think I am a Nazi, please go and never come back." Of himself, he says: "If I suspected my teacher was a Nazi, that's what I would do."[22]

In the SS, Eichmann was used to having vast amounts of control. Few people were in a position to contradict him. His immediate superiors were far away geographically, and those who were the victims of his power stayed invisible at best or were annihilated. The Swedish legation, and particularly Wallenberg, were the exceptions to this pattern, and the experience was a new one for Eichmann.

At one point Wallenberg decided that it might be wise to invite Eichmann and his second-in-command for dinner. Conversation mixed with food and wine would have a greater chance of being effective. The only problem was that Wallenberg, with the busyness of his work of saving Jews, then forgot about the dinner. Only when Wallenberg came home late to two hungry, thirsty, disgruntled guests did he remember. Drinks were mixed quickly and served with an attitude of forced calm that avoided betraying the fact that the most important German in Budapest had been forgotten!

In his quarters in Pest, Wallenberg had neither a cook nor food for such a dinner. However, Lars Berg and Göte Carlsson lived in an elegant home on the Buda side, equipped with a full household staff and an abundance of food. Fortunately for Wallenberg, the cook always insisted on preparing far more food than was needed. On this occasion Wallenberg called Berg on the phone and asked if the guests could be brought there. Wallenberg then announced to Eichmann that dinner itself would be served at the home of another member of the Swedish legation.

Once they arrived, while more drinks were mixed and served, the table was set with the best china and silver. The dinner was such a culinary success that it is unlikely that Eichmann ever knew about the last-minute panic.[23]

After dinner the stage was set for the declaration of diplomatic boundaries that would exist until the end between Wallenberg and the Swedish legation, on the one side, and Eichmann and the Third Reich, on the other. But Wallenberg also articulated the flaws in Nazi beliefs and predicted the by-now-obvious doom of the Reich. Wallenberg broke out of his more natural Swedish reserve and crossed over normal diplomatic boundaries by not only attacking the reasonability of Nazi doctrine but by persuasively threatening Eichmann with his own destruction unless he was willing to stop the killing of the Jews of Hungary.

In a somewhat amazing response, Eichmann replied: "I admit that you're right, Mr. Wallenberg. I actually never believed in Nazism as such but it has given me power and wealth."[24] Then according to Anger, describing Wallenberg's words to him following the dinner, Eichmann went on: "I have this job; and as long as I can enjoy it as I do now—with the women, the champagne, the cognac, the horses, and my palace here in Budapest—I will continue to do so. It is all going to be taken by the Russians. I know that. And I will be shot. But for me there is no salvation, really. If I go on as much as I can with my present job, I

can prolong this for a while. So I'm not going to give in."
Then, in a more threatening tone, he continued: "And I
warn you that you shouldn't try to stop me, because I am
going to do my utmost to work against you. Your diplomatic passport won't help you. And if I find it necessary,
I am going to see that you are liquidated. Accidents can
happen, even to a neutral diplomat!"

Eichmann left the dinner with characteristic charm and
politeness. There was no apparent anger or resentment.
The interchange had been quite blunt and yet civil. Within
days Eichmann attempted to carry out his threat when a
large truck rammed Wallenberg's car. Wallenberg just happened not to be in the car. Furious over the incident, Wallenberg immediately called Eichmann. Eichmann calmly
responded: "I told you that accidents might happen!"[25]
The lines had been clearly drawn on the battlefield of wits
that was to determine the fate of the Jews of Hungary—
a battlefield that was to become the platform for those
three men, each of whom made a difference for good or
for evil.

Raoul Wallenberg in the office of the Swedish legation on November 26, 1944. This may possibly be the last picture taken of Wallenberg before his capture by the Russians in January of 1945. Note the candle, which was on his desk due to frequent blackouts. *(Photographer: Thomas Veres. Courtesy of the United States Holocaust Memorial Museum.)*

A monument honoring Wallenberg was erected in Budapest immediately after the "liberation" but then torn down by the Russians within five days. *(Photographer: Thomas Veres. Courtesy of the United States Holocaust Memorial Museum.)*

102

Hungarian Jewish women are selected for slave labor at Auschwitz, summer of 1944. The great majority of Jews who were not rescued in Hungary ended up in the Auschwitz death camp. *(Photo Credit: Yad Vashem. Courtesy of the United States Holocaust Memorial Museum.)*

Hungarian Jews on the way to the gas chambers. *(Photo Credit: Yad Vashem. Courtesy of the United States Holocaust Memorial Museum.)*

Hungarian Jews waiting to be gassed. *(Photo Credit: Yad Vashem. Courtesy of the United States Holocaust Memorial Museum.)*

In 1956, Hungary revolts against its Russian "liberators." *(Courtesy of Per Anger family.)*

The destruction of the statue of Stalin in Budapest during the 1956 uprising. *(Courtesy of Per Anger family.)*

The Raoul Wallenberg Association demonstrates outside the Soviet Embassy in Stockholm in 1981, demanding the release of Raoul Wallenberg. Per Anger is second on the left, next to Nina Lagergren. The event occurred during the time a Russian submarine was stranded in Swedish waters and might have been traded for Wallenberg instead of just being given back. (*Courtesy of Per Anger family.*)

The Swedish-Russian meeting in Moscow, 1989. At the far end of the table, Nina Lagergren (sister of Raoul), a translator, Guy von Dardel (brother of Raoul), Per Anger, Sonja Sonnenfeld, and three Russian delegates. (*Courtesy of Per Anger family.*)

First page of Raoul Wallenberg's passport returned in 1990 to Wallenberg's family in Sweden. The passport is on loan to the United States Holocaust Memorial Museum and is displayed there. Raoul Gustaf Wallenberg was born on August 4, 1912, in Stockholm, and the passport was issued in Stockholm on June 30, 1944. *(Courtesy of the United States Holocaust Memorial Museum.)*

This is the second page of Raoul Wallenberg's passport. Note Per Anger's signature on the left side. *(Courtesy of the United States Holocaust Memorial Museum.)*

A reception in Stockholm on May 20, 1990. From left to right: Ambassador Per Anger, Israeli Ambassador Moshe Yagar, President of Israel Chaim Herzog, Mrs. Aura Herzog, and His Majesty King Carl XVI Gustaf. *(Courtesy of Per Anger family.)*

6

Battlefield of Wits

Almost fifty years had gone by since the Holocaust in Budapest. Raoul Wallenberg would have been eighty years old, and many who loved him and still sought to find him in the vast Russian prison system came back to Budapest to commemorate his birth. Among those was Kate, who was now a citizen of Sweden.

As Kate looked at some of the museum exhibits reminiscent of those times, she saw an old typewriter from Wallenberg's office. Next to the typewriter lay a piece of paper with names printed on it. To her amazement she saw her grandmother's name and then her uncle's.

It was like going back in a time capsule to a period so remote and yet so real, forever etched in her memory. Once again in her mind's eye Kate was that child of twelve. Her father, she remembered, had been taken to a labor camp in Hungary. There he had died. Her mother had sought the help of a longtime friend, a kindly Swede, Per Anger, to help her with the family's steel company. Her mother, Kate recalled, could no longer be the head of the business because she was Jewish. Kate's mother had been very touched by the kindness of the Swedish diplomat.

Other images passed through her mind. As a child remembers, Kate could still picture herself wearing a gold star. At that time wearing that sacred emblem meant that anyone could kick you, spit at you, and call you names.

From her childhood memory bank, pieces of paper were recalled as important, almost magical. Per Anger had given them one that made them feel more safe. It said they were protected by the king of Sweden. Then another Swede, Raoul Wallenberg, had given her family a beautiful blue and yellow paper with crowns and photographs and important signatures. It was the *Schutzpass,* the "paper of life and death."

Still, in spite of the "paper of life and death," bad things continued to happen. For a short time Kate's family had lived in a house with a yellow star. This meant soldiers could come and take you away just because you were a Jew. Then there was the ghetto, unheated in the coldest winter anyone could remember. To make things worse, before Kate had reached the ghetto, the Arrow Cross had taken the handful of nuts that she had hidden in her pocket, which was more upsetting to her as a child than the fact that they had also taken her shoes. The people inside talked about being blown up by the cannons the soldiers had positioned outside the ghetto.

The memories faded for a moment as the sound of voices around Kate got louder. Then someone she knew greeted her. Then, as she stood alone once again by the old typewriter in Budapest, her thoughts drifted back to the day the ghetto was liberated and the Russian soldiers had given each person a small piece of bread as they left the ghetto. Now, decades later, the walk to her grandmother's house, where they had hidden themselves in the cellar, seemed as clear as if it had been yesterday. She could almost hear the bombs overhead and the sound of gunfire as Russian and German troops fought to the bitter end.

Then a last memory flooded her body with a sense of horror. Russian soldiers had come down the stairs of her grandmother's cellar. They wanted women. They wanted her. Kate's mother had pulled the child's long, loose hair and said, "Look! She's only a child." The soldiers did not understand. They still wanted Kate. Then a woman who had been with them in the cellar showed Kate's mother a fur coat that she had found, which belonged to Kate's grandmother. "If you let me have this coat," she said, "I will take the child's place." The woman left with the soldiers, and once again Kate's life had been saved.

Now in the year 1992, as an adult Kate stood in the place where so much had happened so many years ago and realized once again how grateful she was to the Swedish legation in Budapest.[1]

Until 1944, Hungary had remained in a very unusual position politically: It was an independent country, considered by Germany to be an ally. Hungary maintained a distant friendliness toward Germany; at the same time it feared a takeover by the Soviet Union and hoped for an alliance with the United States. The result was that for most of the war Germany did not include Hungary's Jews in its extermination activities. Until March 1944 when Hitler invaded, the Hungarian Jews resided in relative safety.

The German Reich had encouraged all Europe to believe that Jews were wealthy and, therefore, drained a country of its resources. Contrary to that view:

> In 1930, for example, 4,800 (60.0 percent) of the approximately 8,000 Jewish businessmen lived in one- or two-room apartments. . . . The proportion of poor among the Jews was in fact higher than for the population at large. According to Samu Stern, then head of the Neolog Jewish community, approximately 401,000, or 90 percent,

of the 444,567 Jews [census of 1930] lived at the poverty level. Like 6.9 million other Hungarians in the total population of 8,688,000, they owned neither land nor their own homes. While the Jews constituted 5.1 percent of the population, their proportion among the poor was 5.8 . . . in the business sector, in which Jews represented 43.0 percent: the greatest number of Jewish-owned businesses were small, family-operated ones.[2]

As the war progressed, social and economic sanctions increased, limiting the movement of the Jews and restricting their businesses. As an example of the sanctions, companies were required to have Aryan leaders at the head of their businesses, and it was in this context that many Jewish leaders had already received help from Per Anger.[3]

Hungary was anti-Semitic from way back in its history. Admiral Horthy, regent of Hungary and the leader for most of the war years, was anti-Semitic. This anti-Semitism prepared Hungary for the part it played in the activities of the Third Reich. Yet for the most part, neither Horthy nor the main Hungarian population wanted anything to do with killing Jews. Horthy even allowed himself to be influenced by the Swedish king to cooperate with the rescue of Jews.

Because of the increase in the deportation of Jews from Hungary to certain death, on June 30, 1944, King Gustav V of Sweden sent the following plea to Horthy, a message that was delivered to Horthy by Per Anger:[4]

Having received word of the extraordinarily harsh methods your government has applied against the Jewish population of Hungary, I permit myself to turn to your Highness personally, to beg in the name of humanity that you take measures to save those who still remain to be saved of this unfortunate people. This plea has been evoked by my longstanding feelings of friendship for your country and my sincere concern for Hungary's good name and reputation in the community of nations.[5]

In July Anger sent a dispatch back to Sweden stating that since the king's plea "the government seems to go to great lengths for milder treatment of the Jews."[6] Unfortunately, this change was only temporary.

Because anti-Semitism grows easily under stress, when the real test came and Hitler invaded Hungary in March of 1944, it was easy for the already brutal Nyilas (Arrow Cross or Hungarian Nazis) to join with the German Nazis and become more brutal still. The Nyilas' very roots had been nurtured on hatred for the Jews and jealousy over their supposed economic success. Like a volcano that has waited too long to explode, their anti-Semitism turned vicious. The Nyilas outdid the German Nazis and turned into cheap street thugs who took pleasure in tormenting and killing Jews.

In a dispatch written by Anger to Sweden on July 7, 1944, he graphically described the "brutality and cruelty of the Hungarian local police." His report was based on an eyewitness account from a man visiting a hospital in a little community east of Budapest.

While he was there, the community was surrounded by a couple hundred local police who, after having barred the most important exits, penetrated the houses of the Jews and rallied them together to the town hall square of the community for the quickest possible deportation.

Some of the local police even went into the hospital to seek out Jews. Some of the patients were very sick or recovering from surgery. They were very weak. In spite of protests by the doctors, the police, while hurling insults and curses, dragged the people out of the hospital to join their brothers in despair.[7]

During the summer of 1944 the Nyilas escalated in power as Regent Horthy's ability to keep control of Hungary began to decline. Then in October, Horthy was overthrown and Arrow Cross leader Ferenc Szalasi was established as the new leader. Because it had lost the German Reich's trust, Hungary was now truly a conquered country.

For the average Jew, the change in political power had a very practical result. As one survivor put it, with the German Nazis you would be picked up at any time and taken to the railroad and deported to almost certain death. With the Nyilas, you could be killed immediately in the street.[8]

In August of 1944 Per Anger escorted Elena and baby Birgitta to Sweden and quickly returned to Budapest. For Elena it was to be the start of a nine-month separation that she determined never again to repeat. During the last three months of that time Anger was held captive by the Russians in Hungary and could not communicate with his wife in any way. At home in Sweden, newspapers carried headlines about the bombing of Budapest, making Anger's well-being an issue of constant speculation. For Elena the hardest time may well have been these three months at the end of the war, when she heard nothing from Per and had every reason to believe that he could be dead.

When Anger returned to Budapest, he brought Attaché Lars Berg, Consular Officer Göte Carlsson, and Red Cross representative Asta Nilsson. The small legation on Gellert Hill increased in size a little.

As Hitler became the conqueror of Hungary, new attitudes were required at the Swedish legation. Actions that usually would not have been diplomatically acceptable became necessary, and it created an internal conflict for the members of the legation. Per Anger was, and still is, a man for whom a handshake is as binding as a paper contract. He could not always participate in Wallenberg's disregard for German power. For one thing, Anger's adherence to diplomatic protocol and Swedish neutrality was one of Wallenberg's greatest sources of enablement and protection. Furthermore, the two friends were different from each other, even though they were very compatible. When it came to saving lives, however, Anger and Wallenberg agreed that lives were more important than rules.

For Minister Danielsson the conflict was even greater, for he, too, was a career diplomat, but he was older than Anger and more concerned with proper procedure. Yet even Danielsson became willing to break rules when life and death were involved. Most Swedish passports were not forged, but sometimes a *Schutzpass* would appear where it was obvious that the signature was not authentic. On one occasion, a Swedish official handed a passport to Danielsson and asked him if the signature was his. Danielsson noted that the signature was not his, but before he responded, he asked: "What would happen to the person if my signature were forged?" Informed that the person would be deported to an extermination camp, Danielsson replied that "the signature was authentic."[9]

How serious the consequences could be for the breaking of rules has been underlined by a recent court case in Switzerland. Paul Grueninger, a constable, was convicted in 1940 of falsifying the immigration papers of Jewish refugees fleeing from Austria. By so doing he saved the lives of three thousand Jews. For his "crime" he lost his job and pension, was evicted from his apartment, and was shunned by the community. He died in dishonor in 1982, at the age of eighty. Now, fifty-five years after his conviction, he has been exonerated in the same courthouse in which he had been convicted.

At the time Grueninger saved those Jews, Switzerland had closed its border. "Following orders" was the justification many officials in various countries used for sending Jews back to almost certain death. In Germany alone thirty thousand soldiers were sentenced to death for refusing to fight for the Reich—twenty thousand were executed; others escaped. The exoneration of Grueninger has far-reaching implications for the future. On November 30, 1995, a court said that "following orders" does not justify an action by an official. Officials must take personal responsibility.[10]

The decision made by the Swiss courts is not new.

> After World War II when war criminals were tried at Nuremberg, a new charge was raised in international law: the charge of crimes against humanity. Previously, international law had not dealt with the kinds of atrocities committed during this war. When charged with crimes against humanity, no defendant could claim the protection of having obeyed orders from a superior, though superior orders might be considered by the Tribunal as a mitigating factor in sentencing. The denial of the defense of superior orders has often been called the "Nuremberg Principle."[11]

While Wallenberg was given the authority he needed to function fully as a diplomat, he had been sent for a special mission: to save the Jews. Because he had this specific mission, which lay outside the usual diplomatic venue, it was easier for him to break rules. On the other hand, Anger, the career diplomat, had been trained to do his job in a certain way and was expected to work within the usual diplomatic conventions.

The variations in the roles of the two men, as well as their differences in personality, actually helped to save the Jews of Budapest. Wallenberg ended up with several hundred people helping him directly in rescues that frequently involved the breaking of diplomatic rules, which could have affected the status of Sweden as a neutral nation.

But since rescue efforts depended upon the protective neutrality of the Swedish legation, it was important to function within these rules as often as possible.

Of the two men Anger was the one who kept business going as usual, at least to the public eye. In time of war, neutral legations were only allowed in a foreign country *because* they were neutral. When that neutrality ceased, they were asked to leave. The Swedish legation's job was to help Swedes trapped in a war zone or to aid businesses relating to the country they represented. They could also perform acts of mercy for people in need, regardless of what side those people might be on. Broadly, Anger's tasks fell into two categories. First, he acted as a normal diplomat, giving help where it was needed and providing the neutral front that was necessary if the Swedes, especially Wallenberg, were to stay in Budapest and perform rescues. Second, because he and the other Swedish diplomats were brave and moral men, they took risks and broke rules in order to facilitate the actual rescues.[12]

When he could, Wallenberg played by the rules. He had validated the *Schutzpasses* by negotiating with Regent Horthy to acknowledge them; and while the Swedes were originally allowed to distribute five thousand, eventually they handed out about thirty thousand. The people who held them and who were rescued were lodged in the Swedish safe houses. Toward the end of the war, those rescues were becoming increasingly visible. In spite of the appearance of dividing Wallenberg's work from that of the official legation, eventually the Swedish legation became jokingly called the "Jewish embassy." At the end it is questionable that the neutral front could have convinced anyone much longer.

The organized distribution of passes was only one way Wallenberg and the legation saved lives. More dramatic were some of the rescues of those already chosen for extermination. The following was typical of a Wallenberg rescue:

The Nazis collected Jews and herded them to a brick factory or train station. A waiting boxcar was filled with Jews to be transported to Auschwitz. An official car from the Swedish legation drove up, with a now-too-often-forgotten hero, Vilmos Langfelder, acting as chauffeur. Wallenberg jumped out of the car alone or sometimes with Anger or someone else. He declared himself a neutral diplomat who was there to make sure that there were no Swedish citizens on the train. He bluffed. He threatened to report the German officers to their superiors. Eventually he even threatened them with war crime trials. Since the war had essentially been won already by the Allies, and for months it was known that evidence was being collected for various war crime trials, the threat of such reprisal became an effective deterrent for many. As long as the Germans were in control, rather than the Nyilas, Wallenberg's approach often worked.

Once on the train, Wallenberg barked his orders, sounding very much like a Nazi guard in his boldness and confidence. "All of you who have Swedish passes get off this train!" A few people would show their *Schutzpasses* and leave. Then came the games. "Mr. Levine!" he shouted at a timid-looking man whose name would probably not be *Levine*. "Mr. Levine!" he shouted again. "I saw you yesterday at the legation. Where is the pass I gave you?"

The so-called Mr. Levine would shrink back a little in fear, and whisper, "I don't have a pass." A look of hopelessness would come over his face.

With a confident smile, Wallenberg would shout loudly: "You lost the pass? What a pity. Well, come with me and I will replace the one you lost."

So the rescue would continue until all who had "lost" passes, all who had caught on to the charade and had begun to produce rental receipts or grocery lists that Wallenberg would then recognize as passes, were taken off of the car and brought back to the city under the protection of the Swedish legation.

Most people, however, who were put on trains to be deported were not so lucky. Anger described an incident in a brick factory:

> While I stood there, a train with empty cattle cars was shifted onto a spur that served the brickyard. The doors were opened and as many Jews as possible—men, women, and children—were forced into the cars with kicks and blows. Eighty or so persons were stuffed into each car, which would normally accommodate half as many. A mother tried to hide her child and prevent it being taken along. A soldier saw this, grasped the child by the leg, and flung it into the wagon.[13]

As a token humanitarian gesture, a bucket of water was placed in each wagon, then the doors were closed and nailed shut with boards. The train is said to have steamed around Hungary for a week or so, during which time many died or went insane. Those who survived continued their journey to the gas chambers in Poland.

Sometimes Anger went with Wallenberg; at other times he had to function by himself in a rescue, when more than one place needed help. Wallenberg had a wonderful information system and often found out about people in need from unknown and diverse sources. For example, one day Wallenberg called Anger and explained that he was involved in a rescue and couldn't leave but that there were some people at a railroad station who needed to be rescued. Could Anger go and help them? This time Wallenberg had been warned about a train that was going to take more Jews to Auschwitz.

When Anger arrived at the station, he found the train surrounded by German soldiers. Standing right by the train was the German commander in charge. Using a good amount of ingenuity, Anger walked up to the commander and showed him his passport. "I am a Swedish diplomat," he started. "We as a country have diplomatic relations with Germany, and, by the way, I have close connections with the German ambassador in Budapest," who was Hitler's special envoy.

Anger requested the officer's cooperation in letting him go on the boxcar, but the commander was reluctant. Anger intensified his tactics. "If you don't allow me to go on, then I will report you to your superior, and there will be complications in the diplomatic relationship between Sweden and Germany. We have full diplomatic relations with you. We have our embassy in Berlin, and you have yours in Stockholm. I don't think you should take the risk that I will report this incident," concluded Anger.

At that point Anger was allowed on the train. The usual numbers of people could only show driver's licenses and rental receipts. Only two held real *Schutzpasses.* Anger bluffed, and since on this occasion none of the German soldiers read Hungarian, he managed to take one hundred persons to the Swedish safe houses, with the help of a Hungarian officer who was waiting outside the train. The officer was secretly working for Wallenberg and Anger, motivated by the promise of a letter that would enable the man to settle in Switzerland after the war. Anger kept his word. As Anger put it: "He got a residency in Switzerland, thanks to the fact that he helped the Swedes."[14]

While many of the rescues involved saving groups of people, individuals were also important. A baby was once born in Wallenberg's apartment because no hospital would accept a Jew. Wallenberg was designated as her godfather, and years later she introduced herself to Per Anger after he had delivered a speech.

On another occasion a man told of his efforts to find refuge from the Nazis for his wife and nine-month-old baby. This gentleman was in charge of an International Red Cross Children's Home where, apart from his wife and baby and a few other mothers, most of the children had no mother with them.

One morning some youngsters in Nazi uniforms, carrying rifles, tried to come into the home. The man had papers issued by the Red Cross, the Hungarian Police, and the Hungarian Arrow Cross forbidding anyone from entering the home. The boys seized the papers and tore them up. After they forced their entry, they gave their orders: "Be ready to leave in fifteen minutes!" Overhearing their plans to take the group to the railroad station for deportation and death, the man escaped and hid in the cellar of a neighboring house. After the group of children were taken away, he tore off his yellow star and ran for help. He had heard of the rescues of Raoul Wallenberg, so he ran to his headquarters.

Wallenberg sent out two men but kept the Red Cross man with him, where he would continue to be safe. About an hour and a half later the two men returned with the news that the mothers and babies had been brought to the Budapest ghetto instead of the railway station. The Red Cross man was given some papers by Wallenberg with which he was able to get back his wife and child.[15]

Sometimes one person was saved, sometimes a large group of people. But always, motivating the rescues, was the thought that not only were these meant to be in the name of humanity, they were meant to save a nation.

What looked like the end became the beginning all over again when in October 1944 the Nazis seemed defeated.

Eichmann had been called back to Germany on August 24, deportations had stopped, and even Wallenberg began to make plans to go home for Christmas.

It had been arranged for Swedish women and children still left in Budapest to go home to Sweden for their own safety. The Swedes had been put on board a German troop train. But just before the train was to leave, the loud-speakers announced Hungary, under Regent Horthy, had entered into a cease-fire with the Soviet Union. Anxious to escape before the Russian troops took over, German soldiers put some Swedes off the train so that they could take their seats. Quickly, Anger made sure that the Swedes were given back their seats.

Ultimately, the final decision of whether or not the Swedes should continue on the train was left up to Per Anger. There were some risks. It was possible that, because it carried primarily German soldiers, the train could be shot at or even bombed by the Allies. However, Anger stayed with his original decision to send them home. For a short time some questioned the wisdom of that move.[16]

Then a few hours later, the Horthy regime was officially overturned by the Nazis, and the leader of the Hungarian Nazi Party, Ferenc Szalasi, took Horthy's place as regent.

A survivor of the Holocaust, Agnes Adachi, gives a first-hand account of her memory of the Szalasi takeover.

> I remember the beautiful morning, sunny and cold, when a very excited neighbor of ours ran to us, telling of the BBC announcement that Admiral Nicholas Horthy "Administrator of the Realm" would soon be on the air to announce the break with Germany and that we had joined the Allied forces. My father ran for the champagne. I begged him not to do it, as somehow I would not believe in our great good fortune. He told me I was too young to understand, so he poured the champagne. The Admiral

came on the air. In a few simple words, he announced the intention of the Hungarian Government to break with Germany. He got about that far with his speech, when suddenly he was interrupted by the Nazi anthem and Horthy's voice disappeared. There had been a takeover![17]

After Horthy was deposed, the Arrow Cross began aggressively attacking the Jews, and on October 17 Eichmann returned to renew his final efforts of exterminating the Jewish race. Szalasi was different from Horthy; he had no hesitancy in killing Jews. If the German Nazis had been brutal, to many the Hungarian Nazis seemed even worse. A new reign of terror emerged.

The Hungarian Nazis, who also had less respect for rules than the German Nazis, made the rescue of the Jews much more difficult. Neutral nations were not respected in the same way, and boundaries were crossed that would have been respected before. Safe houses were sometimes plundered, and lives were lost. Some of the Jews who worked directly for Wallenberg were captured and then often rescued once again by the Swedes.

The Nyilas were street thugs, brutal and often sadistic. "Shooting out of eyes, scalping, deliberate breaking of bones and abdominal knife wounds were Nyilas specialties." In one Nyila headquarters, "it was the rule to burn out the eyes of the Jews with red-hot nails before executing them."[18]

> The Jews were constantly mistreated by the Nyilas guards, who often stole their meager provisions. Many of the Jews, including Jewish "foremen commanders," were shot whimsically on flimsy pretexts; this happened, for example, in Dunaharaszti, Pestszentimre, Pécel, and Domony. The number of Jewish casualties was especially high when the companies were marched over the Horthy Miklós bridge in Budapest: the Nyilas soldiers and guards would amuse themselves by shooting straggling Jews into the

Danube. The slaughter assumed such dimensions that special police units had to be called out to protect the Jews from the maddened Nyilas.[19]

One of the most barbaric incidents of the entire Nyila reign was the notorious death march. The Nazis needed labor 120 miles to the west over the Austrian border, but the trains were needed to transport troops. Along with the German Nazis, the Nyilas forced forty thousand Jews to go on foot through the freezing rains to Austria. About 15 to 20 percent did not make it. Those who were judged unfit for work once they reached Austria were pushed back over the border into Hungary, driven into the woods, and left to die of disease, starvation, and exposure to the harsh cold weather.[20]

Anger recalls that there was strong reaction even from the German Nazis to the brutality of the Nyilas in the death march.[21] SS-*Obergruppenführer* and general of the *Waffen*-SS Hans Juttner described these marches:

In November 1944 I made an official tour of inspection of the *Waffen*-SS Divisions fighting in the Hungarian area. In preparation for this tour I had ordered *Obersturmbannführer* [Kurt] Becher to meet me in Vienna. . . . On the evening of my arrival Becher told me that on his journey from Budapest to Vienna he had met columns of Jews marching to the Reich frontier. The march had made a strong impression on him, since the terrible exhaustion of these people was apparent at first sight. At first I would not believe his description, since these things appeared to me almost impossible.

The next morning I drove to Budapest accompanied by Becher and my adjutant. About halfway to Budapest or a little later we met the first columns. Further columns followed at intervals of between 25 and 30 kilometers. As far as I can remember they consisted mainly of women. Unless my memory fails me, all ages up to 60 were represented. . . . The first columns, which had been on the march already for several days, made a truly terrifying impression and confirmed Becher's statement of the day before. Between the individual columns we met stragglers who had been unable to march on and lay in the road ditch. It was at once apparent that they would never be able to march as far as the frontier. These scenes upset me so much that I at once told Becher that immediately after our arrival in Budapest I was going to the Higher SS and Police Leader [Otto Winkelmann] in order to protest sharply against what I had seen on the road. [22]

During this event Wallenberg immediately organized trucks that could bring supplies to those on the road. Later he set up an enormous aid detail using the help of the International Red Cross and the Swedish, Swiss, and Portuguese legations. This included doctors, nurses, nuns, a mobile kitchen that kept food hot, and as much medicine as could be taken. Wallenberg and Anger led the group.[23] Some people were rescued, but for the most part it was a journey of mercy. Supplies were handed out as needed, and if people couldn't be rescued, at least some pain was alleviated.

Per Anger remembers the suffering he saw on that march. It was not easy to watch these people in their agony. As the Swedish diplomatic car drove up to the Austrian border, its blue and yellow flags waving in the air, the driver, who was Jewish, could not control his anger any longer. He had seen too much pain along the way. As they approached the German guards who were sitting around, one of them shouted: "Are you a Jewish swine?" The driver rolled down his window and spat at the guards! By some miracle the Germans let it go. It was just one of many of the times when all of these heroic Swedes and the heroic Jews and Hungarians who worked with them could have been shot on the spot.[24]

By December 1944, the Swedish government had become fully aware of the danger surrounding the Swedish legation in Budapest from both the Arrow Cross and Eichmann. As a result a cable was received from Stockholm, telling the diplomats that if they considered the situation too dangerous they should return to Sweden. During this time, according to Anger, the Swedes were bluffing the Szalasi regime, pretending to recognize their government and promising a place for their ambassador in Stockholm. If the Swedes had left then, the Arrow Cross would have blown up the safe houses, and any Jews left would have been unprotected.

Within the legation they discussed their decision. Minister Danielsson, who had provided stability for the legation throughout the war, asked: "Is there anyone who wants to leave now?" Nobody did. They all stayed on. This decision was particularly remarkable when one realizes that Danielsson was in his midsixties and younger men with his position in other legations had gone home where it was safe.

The legation stood firm when the rest of the world had turned its back. From 1942 on, Sweden, America, and other countries knew of the mass slaughter of Jews at Auschwitz. According to Anger, there was silence from America because of anti-Semitism. Sweden remained silent because that small country was afraid of occupation by the Nazis. But if in 1943, when it was obvious that the Germans were not going to win the war, the newspapers had published what was happening to the Jews and cried out about it, then, according to Anger, the Germans would have thought: *Now that the whole world knows about this, perhaps we have to slow down.* Continued Anger: "The Jewish people themselves would have known that the neutrals knew what was going to happen, and that would have given the Jewish people the courage to fight."[25]

It is right to speak out in the face of evil. To remain silent is neither Christian nor moral. Budapest became the final battlefield of World War II where the fate of God's chosen people Israel was decided. Eichmann got his 600,000, but the Swedes and all who helped them saved 100,000 Jews. Through one stroke of genius alone, Raoul Wallenberg opened the ghetto and saved 70,000 Jews in one day.

In a speech in Illinois, Hugh J. Schwartzberg portrayed most eloquently the blending of Per Anger and Raoul Wallenberg as forces for good that existed in Budapest during those last months of the war. Indeed, until this very day, Anger has made it a lifelong goal to find Wallenberg, who was captured by the Russians as they "liberated" Budapest.

We are here to honor two great men: one who stands as a living flame who is with us here tonight, and one who has lain in the blackness of the Gulag, where he has been rotting, for 43 years. . . .

We who here *speak* can nothing *do* to add to the glory of Anger or of Wallenberg. In a testing time, when they were each in their early 30s (and when that Reich which bragged that it would last for a thousand years lay dying in its 11th and final year) these two, Anger and Wallenberg, stuck their bare hands into that icy dark to extract— and save—some burning embers. . . .

How does a righteous person react when faced with a harm that transcends the possibility of cure? By attempting to do all that is possible. In Wallenberg's words, as repeated by Ambassador Anger, "I'd never be able to go back to Stockholm without knowing inside myself I had done all a man could do to save as many Jews as possible." And in Anger's words, Wallenberg "did all that a man could, to the very last."

... In a righteous cause, the righteous may sometimes have to play by some of their opponents' rules, until those rules can be changed for the better. So Anger and Wallenberg bent every diplomatic rule in the rule book. When Wallenberg arrived in Budapest, he found that Anger had already used provisional passports, visa certificates, Red Cross protection letters. It was to this arsenal that Wallenberg added the *Schutz-passes,* the protective passports, those pieces of paper whose three blue and yellow crowns served to help rescue 25,000 of the perhaps 100,000 that these figures helped pluck out of the butcher's ice-box, alive.

... [Much later, when the campaign to free Wallenberg from the Gulag had begun] Ambassador Anger understood that the Russians will on occasion respond to force or to advantage secured through negotiation. Ambassador Anger suggested early on that prisoner exchange was a language which the Russians understood. He understood that nations might bargain for Wallenberg's return, but it was a time when Anger himself found his audience would not listen.

[He teaches us] ... that some causes must be fought over and over, year after year. Some tasks cannot be laid down. ...

The people of Sweden stand tall in this portion of history not just because of Raoul Wallenberg, not just because of you, Ambassador Anger, but also because of others' names which you have felt deserving. ... But you and Wallenberg were particularly special. Elie Wiesel spoke for all Jews when he said of Raoul Wallenberg, "He is a man embodying our thirst for justice and dignity, our quest for humanity." And you, Mr. Ambassador, you also were a shining light in the cold black of the Nazi dark.

Camus taught us that some men find it possible to fight evil only during the plague years. You have taught us that there are a few who can spend a lifetime in the struggle for human rights.

130

Tales like yours are meant for retelling. In some unknown future, children not yet born will learn from your example what it can mean to be human. I cannot believe that their worlds will be free from evil, but I can be certain that their flames, which you have helped to spark, will illumine some other darkness.[26]

7

Mr. Ambassador

During the last days of the American involvement in Vietnam, war correspondent Ed Bradley described his escape from Saigon, shortly before it became Ho Chi Minh City. In a television interview Bradley admitted: "It was a city that I thought I . . . might not get out of. It was a city in total chaos.

"There were desperate scenes with families separated and crying out for help, pleading not to be left behind. Helicopters were landing on the roof and inside the compound as we walked to the back of the embassy."

As they attempted to enter the American embassy, they had to fight their way through the crowds and ultimately scale a wall. Marines on the top of the wall kept the crowds back.

Once over the wall, Bradley saw some embassy employees dumping money in barrels and then burning it in order to keep the enemy from getting it.

"Then," said Bradley, "I made my way to the top floor of the American Embassy. I walked out into that darkened hallway and saw the light from the ambassador's conference room at the end of the hallway. And I said, 'My God, that's the light at the end of the tunnel!'"[1]

In any country when people are stranded and without direction, an embassy can truly become the "light at the end of the tunnel." For its citizens, it can provide a way of escape; it can provide direction for those seeking medical help; it can become a place of asylum; it can help in locating missing people or stolen property.

Per Anger was once asked: "What does a diplomat really do besides giving or going to receptions and dinners?" He replied facetiously: "It is sometimes said that a diplomat's work consists to a large extent to report home to his foreign office in code and secret messages what most of the news reporters have cabled their papers in open language the day before."[2]

His own diplomatic career, however, contradicts such a mistaken view of diplomatic service. Even after the unusual circumstances and challenges of World War II Budapest, Anger's ongoing commitment to duty and to helping people is a textbook example of the importance and practical value of foreign embassies and their hard-working employees.

Following the Russian liberation, Anger and the other diplomats had been either on the run or held in captivity. After being held by the Russians for three months, Anger returned home to Sweden on April 18, 1945. One of the greatest disappointments of his life was to find that his friend Raoul Wallenberg had not returned earlier, as he hoped.

Anger took a brief period to rest. Then he worked at the foreign office in Stockholm, during which time his second child, Jan, was born. Anger's stay in Sweden was short-lived, however. He was candid about his opinion of the Russians and his belief that they were holding Wallenberg, a view that was not popular within a foreign office concerned with maintaining warm relations with the Soviet Union.

Even before Anger had reached Swedish soil, as he traveled home by way of the Soviet Union, he had been met by the Swedish ambassador in Moscow, Staffan Söderblom, and warned: "Remember, when you get home to Sweden—not one harsh word about the Russians!"[3] Partly as a result of his unwillingness to obey that order, Anger was relocated to Cairo, Egypt, where he served from 1946 to 1948 as secretary at the embassy.

In Cairo, Anger once again played the role of the humanitarian. When an epidemic of cholera broke out, he reacted by immediately mobilizing Sweden to send medicines, vaccines, and clothing. It was always the obligation of the embassy to be prepared to give immediate aid when crisis arose in the country in which it was located.[4]

During this time, Swedish relations with Ethiopia fell under the jurisdiction of the Cairo embassy. The Swedish presence in Ethiopia itself was limited to just one chargé d'affaires in Addis Ababa. When the chargé d'affaires in Ethiopia went on leave, Anger was sent to replace him for a few months. There, in a relatively obscure Third World country, far from the capitals of Europe, Anger found himself for the first time since Budapest face-to-face with the Soviets in their huge Addis Ababa embassy. In spite of his mixed feelings, he managed to maintain a correct relationship with them.

Returning to Sweden in 1948, Anger was directed to head the Swedish task force investigating the fate of Wallenberg. By now the Swedish government could no longer deny that Wallenberg was possibly being held a prisoner by the Soviets. Anger remained in Sweden for five years at the political department and in the foreign office.[5]

There was, however, a lack of aggressiveness in the Swedish government's approach toward finding Wallenberg. As was symbolized by Söderblom's warning to

Anger, Sweden had a cautious relationship with the Soviet Union over the Wallenberg case. Sweden was too close geographically and too small to risk offending. Added to this was the interdependence that Sweden has always had economically with the Soviets. These factors, coupled with a seemingly united reluctance among the Swedes to aggressively confront, to negotiate a trade of spies for Wallenberg, and certainly to threaten any reprisals, explain some of the difficulties Anger encountered with the Swedish government in his efforts to find Wallenberg. As Anger describes it, "I took a great risk there when I said that I can't go on any longer with the Raoul Wallenberg case because I don't see eye-to-eye with the government."

Anger's difference with his own government was too clear-cut to be ignored. Indeed, Swedish Foreign Minister Undén seemed to be perfectly willing to accept the notion that Wallenberg was not on Russian territory. During Anger's continued work on the Wallenberg case in the years 1949–50, he noticed that Undén maintained his negative attitude. Then at the end of 1950 Anger had a chance to speak directly with Undén while they traveled together. Anger explained his reasons for believing that the Russians were holding Wallenberg, and he urged Undén to exchange one of several spies whom Sweden was holding for the release of Wallenberg. Undén's cold reply was: "The Swedish government does not do such things." In January of 1951 Anger asked to be relieved of handling the Wallenberg case.[6]

Fortunately, Anger enjoyed support within the foreign office and was able to continue his diplomatic career. Though it wasn't easy for him to keep silent when he felt so strongly about the case, he realized dramatic gestures—like ending his diplomatic career—would not help his old friend. "I wouldn't help anyone if I sort of stopped my career, went out on the street and said, 'I disagree with the Swedish government because they don't do enough for Raoul Wallenberg.' It would only have led to my losing my job and not being able to do anything."[7]

In 1953 Anger was named first secretary to the embassy in Paris; there his third child, Peter, was born. Anger was assigned to the trade section, an area of interest to him ever since Berlin. Compared to the dangerous situations he had been in previously, Paris was tranquil. When not attending to import-export issues, Anger spent much of his time officiating at the weddings of resident and traveling Swedes, so much so that he was once asked, "How does the Pastor like to live in Paris?"[8]

In 1955 Anger was named counselor to the embassy in Vienna, Austria, specifically in charge of trade affairs. A year later, in the fall of 1956, the uprising took place in Hungary. For a few short days Hungary was free, an event symbolized by mobs pulling down the statue of Stalin in the park and then systematically shattering it into pieces. Abruptly, a few days after it began, the freedom was ruthlessly crushed by the Red Army. Once again the ending of the war in Hungary, ten years earlier, was to affect Per Anger's life and career.

In the autumn of 1944 the future of Hungary had been at stake in the determination of which of the Allied forces were allowed to liberate Hungary. Churchill tried to organize a secondary attack on the Balkans, but Stalin prevented him from doing so, and Roosevelt supported Stalin.

In his victory broadcast on May 13, 1945, Winston Churchill warned:

> On the continent of Europe we have yet to make sure that the simple and honorable purposes for which we entered the war are not brushed aside or overlooked in the months

following our success, and that the words "freedom," "democracy," and "liberation" are not distorted from their true meaning as we have understood them. There would be little use in punishing the Hitlerites for their crimes if law and justice did not rule, and if totalitarian or police Governments were to take the place of the German invaders.[9]

Responsible people throughout the world foresaw what was going to happen if the Russians liberated Eastern Europe: The British saw it, the Hungarians saw it, the Russians saw it, and—perhaps first of all—the Nazis saw it. Only the Americans seemed blind. Roosevelt may have seen it, too, but he was not willing to endanger Stalin's so-called goodwill and his promised participation in the war against Japan by crossing his path. Chester Wilmot comments: "Roosevelt apparently accepted almost with equanimity the prospect of Russia dominating the Continent, since he genuinely believed that friendliness and frankness on his part would be met by an equally sympathetic response from Stalin."[10]

Another possible motive could have been that it was also an election year, and Roosevelt may not have wanted to be seen as pleasing the British, since the Balkans were considered to be a part of that interest.

In reality, Churchill's fears were well founded. In his famous "iron curtain" speech delivered in 1946 at a college in Missouri, Churchill shocked Americans by stating for the first time that the Soviet Union could become a dangerous adversary.

From Stettin in the Baltic to Trieste in the Adriatic, an iron curtain has descended across the Continent. Behind that line lie all the capitals of the ancient states of Central and Eastern Europe. Warsaw, Berlin, Prague, Vienna, Budapest, Belgrade, Bucharest and Sofia—all these famous cities and the populations around them lie in what I must call the soviet sphere. This is certainly not the liberated Europe we fought to build up. Nor is it one which contains the essentials of permanent peace.[11]

In Hungary the Russian "liberation" became enforced Communist rule. "First 'people's courts' purged influential Hungarians likely to oppose Communist rule. Shortly thereafter the police and gangs of toughs cooperated to force opposing political parties out of business. By 1948, the Communists were firmly in control and all opposition had vanished."[12]

For Hungary, the Stalinization of Europe started in Budapest with the rape of women and young girls. This went on for four years, ending in 1949. Later, in interviews with Freedom Fighters and other Hungarian citizens, it became clear that the roots of the uprising against Russian rule started in the terrible acts committed against the Hungarian people during that so-called liberation. "I saw too much in 1945," they would say.

The savage behavior of the Russian troops in Budapest, and all over the county, the indiscriminate shooting parties, the looting and the endless rape shocked the population deeply. It was something they never forgot nor forgave. But it was not only the behavior of the troops that appalled the Hungarians. Terrible as this was, people might have understood and even found forgiveness in their hearts. After all, these soldiers had gone through the most dreadful experiences, had faced death many times, and might die in battle next day; the Hungarians also knew that Khirgiz and Mongol troops did not stand on a high level of civilization and, after some time had passed, they might have accepted these things as "regrettable excesses." But the Russians and Communists never allowed this to happen. It was, indeed, their stupidity, inherent in the system, which, right from the beginning, spoiled relations between the Russians and the Party on one hand and the people on the other. No, there were no "regrettable excesses"; all the stories about the Russians not behaving like perfect gentlemen in an English club were, according to the Russians and the Hungarian Communists, the dastardly slanders of reactionary elements and Hitlerite Fascist beasts. To speak of "regrettable excesses" meant to accept these looting and raping stories as true; to "forgive" and "understand" meant to accuse—in other words to side with the enemies of the new democratic regime and the "glorious liberating Red Army," as the Russian army always had to be referred to, for short.[13]

Hungary's "liberation" resulted in the exchange of one dictator for another. As one survivor stated: "Little did we know that our 'liberation' would be by an even greater and more lasting enemy—the Soviet Union."[14] Many have said that if the German Nazis were cruel, the Nyilas were worse, and if the Nyilas were worse, the Red Army was still worse. Even though anti-Semitism remained in the Hungarian culture, "Anti-Semitism was not a live issue in the revolution. Russia was the common enemy and nothing else counted."[15]

Lars Berg testified to the Russian atrocities when he wrote a book about the activities of legation members during the last days of the war and the "liberation." Originally called *What Happened in Budapest,* it is now available in English under the title *The Book That Disappeared: What Happened in Budapest.* It first came out in Swedish and was published in Sweden in 1949.

Berg's book contains graphic descriptions of the atrocities of the Russian troops. It is perhaps one of the most detailed eyewitness accounts available. Years ago, when the book was published in Sweden, it disappeared from all the bookstores in one day. How that happened is open to speculation. However, once again, one must always keep in mind the geographical and economic vulnerability of a small country like Sweden bordered by a large, aggressive country like Russia.

When the Russian troops came into Hungary, they had no regard for neutral nations, no respect for the rights of ownership, and no concern for human suffering. Author Martin Caidin describes the mentality of the Russian soldier, based on a study of the Battle of Kursk in World War II, and centered also on studies prepared by the United States Department of the Army. He quotes from those military studies and claims, "It is possible to predict from experience how virtually every soldier of the western world will behave in a given situation—but not the Russian. The characteristics of this semi-Asiatic, like those of his vast country, are strange and contradictory."[16] In general the report goes on to describe the Russian soldier as unpredictable: capable of great kindness and great cruelty, unafraid of his own destruction, with a contempt for human suffering and even death itself, both for himself and for his victim.[17]

Berg tells bizarre stories of how the troops randomly ravaged houses in a city where devastation was already nearly complete. Besides stealing valuables, they would do inappropriate things like smash toilet bowls and then relieve themselves on a soft carpet. In Berg's own apartment the Russians broke in one cold night. After smashing up good furniture, they built a fire with it on top of a valuable Persian rug and in front of a perfectly usable fireplace.

What was worse by far than the abuse of possessions was the abuse of human beings. No woman was safe. The only "safe" ones were those who had already connected with some officer who might keep them from the others. When soldiers decided to rape a woman in her own house, the husband was allowed to stay as long as he did not interfere.

Perhaps the most terrible fate of all was that which occurred to young girls, virgins, chosen from throughout Budapest for their beauty. When a new girl was brought in to the soldiers, they all watched as this girl who had never been naked before a man in her life was now undressed in front of them. Then she was taken from bed to bed until she fainted. If she survived this first ordeal, she was taken on as passable, but she was not allowed to dress again. She cleaned, mended clothes, and in general worked for the troops until once again she was used for sex. A few of these girls stole clothes from the men and escaped. Such was true of the girl who told Lars Berg the above story. However, she was pregnant by the time she escaped, and after giving this information, she killed herself.

In the Red Army, women were considered to be excellent soldiers, equal to or superior to men. Their behavior supported this reputation. In Budapest in 1945 young boys, like young girls, were not safe. Many young boys were literally grabbed off the streets and put into trucks where they were sexually attacked by these women. Seminarians were especially desirable.[18]

Anger describes a memory of the Soviet "liberation" on the eve of leaving for a time of enforced captivity with the Russians in Hungary.

During the day, a great number of Russian units of distinctly lower quality arrived. We came through all right because of our guards and now understood how lucky we had been. As a matter of fact, we had been miraculously saved. All around us, new troops were marching in, the last pockets of resistance were cleared out, and chaos reigned. Women's screams, the death-rattles of dying men, the chattering of machine guns, the smoke of burning habitations—everything spun together into a ghastly cacophony I shall never forget.[19]

No wonder that ten years after the Russians entered Hungary, the memories were fresh and the desire to escape the tyranny of the Russians was strong. Floods of refugees, about 150,000 to 200,000 of them, poured over the Austrian border. Many countries took in some of these people.

Sweden had a quota of five thousand, so characteristically Anger selected those who were sick and dying. This was in contrast to other countries that were much more concerned with the refugees' work qualifications. With the exception of Austria and Sweden, countries conducted medical examinations and considered age as well as economic usefulness. For example, a family of seven were examined by United States officials. The father and five children were admitted to the United States, but the mother was rejected after it was discovered that she had a patch on her lung. Yet at the Austrian border there was no immigration officer "turning back Hungarian refugees if they had a patch on the lung. The mentally sick, people with venereal or the worst infectious diseases were let in and made welcome."[20]

Along with Austria, the Swedes felt differently. Anger said simply, in the low-key way he has when he speaks of himself, "It was a more humanitarian way of doing it." Many of the refugees recovered well, and some became functioning citizens in Sweden.[21]

Returning to Sweden in 1957, Anger spent the next four years as head of personnel in the foreign office. It was the sort of desk job that Anger normally did not relish—a task characterized by "low salary and harder work." Nonetheless, he found this job both challenging and important. "You had to see to it that the right person was transferred to the right post," he explained.

Among other things, this meant taking the diplomat's family situation into consideration as well as his personality and character. "That was very, very challenging, and you sometimes succeeded, and you were very satisfied that you had been of some help." The repercussions of a bad decision could be tremendous, with all kinds of personality conflicts occurring in embassies with the wrong mixture of personnel. No doubt Anger's experiences in Budapest made him particularly appreciative of the necessity of embassy personnel working together in harmony.

Toward the end of this period in Stockholm, Anger discovered the consul general in San Francisco would be retiring, leaving that post vacant. Anger suggested that he pay a visit to San Francisco, as no one from the foreign office had made an inspection there in some time. Upon his arrival, Anger immediately fell in love with the city. However, his knowledge of the politics of the foreign office told him that if he appeared too eager, he wouldn't get the assignment. Therefore, he downplayed his enthusiasm. One day the foreign minister remarked that no one seemed to want the San Francisco post, then fixed his gaze on Anger. Feigning surprise, Anger announced he was available, and off he went in the fall of 1961.

Anger's predecessor had become bogged down in assisting with the complicated inheritance problems that occurred when a Swedish immigrant to America left an inheritance to relatives in the home country. Anger wanted to make something more of the consul general's position, which dealt with trade relations and helping Swedish citizens. He saw a potential for international trade, which is terribly important for Sweden, as the country's economy rests on its exports. In San Francisco in the early sixties, the California economy was booming. It represented a tremendous market for Swedish exporters.

Anger's opportunity came with the 1963 World's Fair in Seattle. Initially Sweden, Denmark, and Norway balked at the expense and declined to participate. Then Anger heard rumors that the Danes were making secret plans to send a delegation after all. Anger realized if he waited for the Swedish government to react, he might be too late to reserve adequate space. On his own initiative, he booked a pavilion, a move that the Swedish government endorsed shortly thereafter, to his relief.

The Swedes not only showed up for the World's Fair, but they did so with a flair. For it was the brainstorm of a particularly inventive Swedish trade commissioner to open the fair by shooting the famed Swedish *Vasa* cannon. Over three hundred years old, this relic came from the *Vasa,* a ship sunk in 1628 in the Stockholm harbor during the reign of Gustavus Adolphus, the famous Swedish warrior king. The *Vasa* had been raised from the harbor only a few years prior to the World's Fair, and one of its few surviving cannon had been restored to use.

On the opening day of the World's Fair, the Swedish trade commissioner dressed up in a uniform similar to that worn by Swedish soldiers in the 1630s. With Anger, visiting dignitaries, and the citizens of Seattle watching, the man set off the cannon—with a blast so strong that it tipped over a Danish hot dog stand.

The attention the *Vasa* cannon generated was not lost on Anger, who quickly made plans for what he called "Operation West Coast." This involved transporting the cannon around the West Coast, using it to inaugurate a series of "Sweden Weeks" in various cities, including San Francisco, Los Angeles, San Diego, Portland, and Phoenix. These events promoted Swedish trade and culture. Anger made full use of his diplomatic skills, enlisting the cooperation of the local governments involved. He also enjoyed the support of the United States Air Force, whose high-ranking officers were fascinated by the cannon and offered to fly it around the United States without cost to Sweden.

The first "Sweden Week" in San Francisco was particularly impressive. Anger had arranged for Prince Bertil to fly out from Sweden to participate in a ceremony outside the mayor's office. Standing on his balcony, alongside Anger and Prince Bertil, the mayor formally proclaimed "Sweden Week" in San Francisco. The *Vasa* cannon was set off, and a military band struck up the United States' and Sweden's national anthems. Afterwards, Prince Bertil drove around in a Volvo, opening seven different Swedish exhibits throughout the city. That week in San Francisco even the cable cars flew the Swedish flag.

After Anger spent four years in San Francisco, the foreign office approached him regarding an ambassadorship in Brazil. The offer was tempting, but Anger felt he had not finished in San Francisco. The Sweden Weeks had only just begun, and Anger was reluctant to walk away just as his efforts were gathering momentum. Characteristically, Anger stayed on in San Francisco for one more year, but at a price—returning to Sweden, he was told there were no posts abroad for him.

Once more, Anger became the humanitarian. Named head of the foreign aid department, Anger held that position for four years. He traveled extensively among the Third World nations of Asia and Africa and participated as a delegate to the United Nations' meetings in New York, Geneva, and Vienna. It was a tough job. Within Sweden, a fierce debate was waged among the political parties over the direction and scope of the programs. At times Anger found himself squeezed between conflicting philosophies. Moreover, he was often at odds with misguided policies. "I was very frustrated over the meaningless way of giving away money which only hurt people in the long run," Anger explained. Giving money alone, without guidance, was not enough. Later on in his retirement years, Anger would work on foreign aid projects that took a different approach.

In 1970 Anger became an ambassador. Posted to Australia, he spent five years organizing visits of Swedish trade missions and initiating annual conferences of Swedish industrialists. In the midst of this routine diplomatic activity, Anger had more than one occasion to display his old resourcefulness.

For instance, Sweden has a highly developed mining industry with a number of major companies producing mining equipment for export all over the world. Australia has tremendous mineral deposits and a highly developed mining industry of its own. Thus, it was natural that representatives of Swedish mining-equipment manufacturers would approach Anger to ask if he might be able to open the Australian market to their products. Anger set out to arrange a visit from a Swedish delegation. However, the Australian government rebuffed his efforts. As he recounts it, they said: "We have had so many sales delegations here, we are not really interested."

Anger responded that actually the Swedes were very impressed with Australian mining techniques and were simply interested in studying their methods. It was a matter of specialists coming to compare notes with other specialists, he explained. "They swallowed that," Anger now notes wryly.

So Anger led a Swedish delegation through the mining districts of Australia. To maintain the ruse that the purpose of the trip was entirely informational, Anger arranged for Swedish geology professors to accompany the delegation. To the business people he said, "Keep quiet and hide yourselves." Anger opened every meeting, describing the good relationship that existed between the Australians and the Swedes and in general doing all he could to get the hosts relaxed. Then a Swedish professor would discuss the state of underground mining in Sweden. This would, inevitably, prompt the question: "But sir, what kind of equipment do you use?" In response, one of the businessmen would screen a film displaying Swedish equipment. Suddenly the Australians were interested. Anger encouraged rounds of toasts and singing. By the end of a typical evening, he relates, "The Australians got so enthusiastic that they put down their orders on the paper napkins nearby."

With similar ingenuity Anger used sports as a device with which to establish common ground between Sweden and Australia. Sweden was a pioneer in *orientering*—a sport where, with the help of a map and a compass, you run through terrain in the shortest possible time.

Two Swedish brothers who were active in *orientering* and were also compass salesmen asked Anger to help introduce the sport in Australia so they could sell their products on the Australian market. Through Anger's initiative, the brothers came to Australia, and the sport was introduced. Clubs were formed, and Anger became an honorary member of one of them. The Swedish word *orientering* was now spelled with two *e*s: *orienteering*. The English language was thus enriched with another Swedish word.[22]

His time as ambassador to Australia ended in 1975, and Ambassador Anger next set his eyes on Canada. The position was not open, but he was promised he would have it within a year. In the meantime, he was named inspector general of the Swedish foreign missions in the Middle East, North Africa, and South Europe. His job was to travel to Swedish embassies in those regions and see what he could do for their staff. He evaluated "their salary situation and their health care as well as how they cooperated between themselves and the working conditions at the embassy." It was the type of hands-on job Anger found interesting.

Anger finished his diplomatic career as ambassador to Canada, a country that was very similar to Sweden in terms of climate and raw materials, and hence an important trading and diplomatic partner. Anger organized the first Swedish industrial conferences in Canada and introduced Swedish commercial delegations to western Canada.

Canadians very often competed with Swedes in sports, especially in ice hockey. At many events Anger threw the puck at the start of the games. Curling was another sport in which the two countries had a common interest. At the 1978 world championship in Canada, the Canadians won over the Swedes. At the concluding banquet in a clubhouse by the rink, Anger was asked to lead the Swedish team in a friendly farewell game. The guests, dressed in black tie, stepped down to the rink. Anger, who had never curled before, was to throw the first stone. He quickly requested some instructions from the Swedish leader and started the game. Anger's stone stopped in the middle of the house— beginner's luck. The Canadians were so impressed they asked Anger if he would like to join their club.[23]

During his time in Canada, Anger started to work for the release of Wallenberg by writing the first draft of his book *With Raoul Wallenberg in Budapest*. Canadians became interested in the Wallenberg cause. One of the first Raoul Wallenberg associations was established in Edmonton, Alberta, by the Swedish honorary consul Lars Fahlstrom. He had very good contact with some members of the Canadian Parliament and worked hard for the Wallenberg cause. The question was raised about the possibility of making Wallenberg an honorary citizen of Canada.

While in Ottawa, Anger was invited to be present at one session of Parliament when Wallenberg was going to be honored. Anger stood to acknowledge the tribute paid to his friend, and he was overwhelmed when the members of Parliament rose to give him a standing ovation.

In December 1979, when Anger was leaving his post in Canada, his colleagues in the Canadian foreign office honored him at a farewell luncheon. In their good-bye speech, to his great joy, they informed Anger that the Canadian government *had* decided to make Wallenberg an honorary citizen of Canada.[24] It was an appropriate ending to Anger's forty years of diplomatic service for his country.

Anger's retirement years have been no less active than the one's preceding them. As director of the Raoul Wallenberg Association, Stockholm, a position he began in January 1980, he has traveled every continent lecturing, speaking, and working for the release of Raoul Wallenberg.

Anger continues to work on humanitarian issues. For a period he sat on a committee in Stockholm that awarded prizes to inventors who developed useful inventions for helping Third World countries. The idea was to free the citizens of Third World countries from a reliance upon cheap Western manufactured goods and to stimulate their own innovations. Many of the best designs were collected in a book that was distributed throughout the Third World, giving each country access to the ideas and inventions of the other countries. The project's strong emphasis on self-sufficiency was particularly attractive to Anger, who had seen the futility of simply throwing money at a problem during his years as head of Swedish foreign aid.

During this period Anger became involved in another foreign aid project that also stressed practical self-sufficiency. Officials from the Chinese embassy had approached the Swedes, asking if retired Swedish business people were available to travel to China for a short time and give advice on running factories and other management issues. Ambassador Anger helped circulate this request among the members of the Retired People's Association of Sweden. The response was incredible; hundreds of engineers and executives stepped forward. Since these retirees were receiving pensions from the Swedish government, they could afford to volunteer.

All involved benefited. The Chinese were thrilled to receive such expertise at little cost to themselves, and Swedish Foreign Aid officials could bask in the success of a project that didn't cost their country very much either. Swedish industry was equally delighted; their retired managing directors were in a position to direct business toward their former firms. More important, perhaps, the effort gave scores of Swedish retirees a reason to feel useful again. Indeed, the venture's success prompted a Swedish discussion of making greater use of the country's elderly citizens.

Increasingly, Anger stressed the message that one person can make a difference. Furthermore, he never at any time relinquished his goal of someday finding Raoul Wallenberg. "I always had in my mind as soon as I finish my job, as soon as I retire, I will concentrate all my efforts on the Raoul Wallenberg case." At another time Anger explained: "The Raoul Wallenberg case has always been in the back of my mind. I've lived with it in a way over all those years. . . . But my intention the whole time was that as soon as I got into retirement I would work on it full time."

After his retirement, Anger joined the Swedish Raoul Wallenberg Association. He became a member of its board, with Raoul's half sister and half brother, Nina Lagergren and Guy von Dardel. Sonja Sonnenfelt, the driving force in the Stockholm office, was also a member. In 1986 Anger was elected chairman.[25]

In the light of increased awareness of Wallenberg's fate, due to new testimonies that he might still be alive somewhere in the Soviet Union, the association started its drive to get the world's support for his release.

During the next fifteen years Anger traveled repeatedly throughout Europe as well as to the United States, Canada, Australia, and Israel, bringing the Wallenberg story to the world's attention. Now he could speak more freely, without the restrictions of the Swedish foreign office.

Wherever he went, Anger met Jewish people who had been saved by Wallenberg and who expressed their deep gratitude for the Swedish legation's rescue work. He found survivors all over the world and had many moving meetings with them. He gained a perspective of how great the Wallenberg rescues had been.

Raoul Wallenberg associations were formed in most countries, including Australia, the United States, and Canada, with the help of many dedicated persons. These associations became valuable supporters in spreading the knowledge about Wallenberg's deeds and in pushing the governments of their countries to help find Wallenberg.

At the end of 1979, in the House of Representatives in Washington, D.C., Anger made the first of the hundreds of speeches on the subject. The speech was recorded in the *Congressional Record*.

In the early eighties, Anger spoke in San Francisco to a full auditorium, with many Jewish survivors present. Among them was Ivan Szekely, one of Wallenberg's drivers. He had driven Wallenberg and Anger during their rescue work on the death march from Budapest to the Austrian border. It was a happy reunion.

On this occasion he also renewed his friendship with Annette and Tom Lantos, who were saved by Wallenberg and are among the most dedicated persons working for the Wallenberg cause. They had met in the sixties, when

Anger was Swedish consul general in San Francisco. Professor Lantos often came to the consulate with groups of students who wanted to learn about Sweden before going there on a study trip. When Anger met the couple again, Tom Lantos was running for Congress. On their initiative and through Congressman Lantos's relentless efforts for Wallenberg's recognition in Congress and elsewhere, Wallenberg was granted the rare honor of honorary citizenship by the United States.

Tom and Annette Lantos have also visited Sweden many times. On one occasion Congressman Lantos led a delegation from America to Stockholm to honor Wallenberg. On a Raoul Wallenberg Day, which is on January 17, in the cathedral of Stockholm, Congressman Lantos made a most moving speech about Wallenberg. Members of the Swedish government and foreign ambassadors assigned to Sweden were present.[26]

Anger continued during these years to bring Wallenberg's cause to public attention as he spoke in churches, synagogues, schools, universities, clubs, and conferences. He appealed to governments and parliaments to support the Swedish efforts to have Wallenberg released.

In the process Anger developed important contacts with some heads of state. According to Anger, when Gorbachev visited Stockholm in 1990, the foreign office arranged for Anger to have a meeting with him regarding Wallenberg. Gorbachev's reaction to the plea for help in finding Wallenberg was not positive. The explanation for his negative attitude was discovered later: At that time he had no power over the KGB.[27]

Soviet resistance to cooperation in the search for Wallenberg was graphically illustrated in San Remo, Italy, in 1983. A Swedish worldwide symposium honoring Alfred Nobel was arranged in cooperation with the Italians. Scientists from all over the world attended, among them thirty Nobel laureates. Anger was invited to lecture about Wallenberg and his mission in Budapest.

When he arrived and read the printed program, Anger discovered that he was going to speak on the subject "Science and Peace." Astonished, he asked the Italian professor responsible for the program why this change of subject. The answer was: "Of course I know that you are going to talk about Wallenberg, but I did not put that in as I want the official Soviet delegation to be present."

Anger started his speech. The message moved many in the auditorium, especially the Jewish scientists. But when Anger described how Wallenberg had been arrested by the Soviets, most of the Soviet delegates stood up and left. Only one young Soviet scientist remained seated taking notes.

After the lecture, this man asked one of Anger's colleagues at the Nobel Foundation for a private talk. The Russian said: "It was wonderful to listen to this outspoken speech. We need much more of that because we have so many like Wallenberg who are disappearing in the Gulag."

The Italian professor who had scheduled Anger's speech was so taken by the story that he included portions of the speech at the concluding ceremony, which took place on the last day in the presence of the Swedish king and the Italian president. The Wallenberg story therefore became the main message the scientists took back with them.

In the fall of 1989, Nina Lagergren, Guy von Dardel, Sonja Sonnenfelt, and Per Anger were invited to Moscow to receive some of Wallenberg's belongings. The Soviet representatives could not, however, prove that he had died, and they denied that there were any existing documents about him. Two years later, after the coup, an official Swedish-Russian commission was formed. The archives were opened, and the commission obtained over one hundred documents about Wallenberg. So far, however, none tell what really happened to him.[28]

In June 1995, Anger was invited to visit German president Roman Herzog in Bonn. The visit had been initiated by Max Grünberg, who had been working in Canada for the Raoul Wallenberg Association and now had settled in Israel. The president asked Anger what Germany could do to help. Anger stressed the importance of German support to encourage the Russians to make greater efforts to find out what had happened to Wallenberg. So far the Russians have not proved that Wallenberg died. Consequently, the Swedes believe he still might be alive somewhere in the former Soviet Gulag. President Herzog promised to see what could be done.[29]

One important source of information regarding Wallenberg has been created by the media. Documentary films have been made in many countries and have been based on interviews with a variety of people, including his own family members and colleagues like Per Anger.

In Anger's opinion, the greatest media impact for Wallenberg, however, came from the Hollywood film *Wallenberg*. Per Anger was asked to read a prologue and an epilogue for this production.

A number of well-written books and articles have also promoted knowledge of Raoul Wallenberg and have helped to keep alive the search for information regarding his fate. Yet there is no doubt that without the efforts of Anger and others like him, followed by the work within the different Raoul Wallenberg associations, the world would not have known much about Wallenberg's heroism and ultimate imprisonment. Worldwide support started to show results only after the perestroika and, even more so, after Boris Yeltsin took over.[30]

As in any story of great proportions, interpretations and even facts regarding the fate of Wallenberg are questionable at times. On May 13, 1996, *U.S. News and World Report* published an article relating to Wallenberg entitled "The Angel Was a Spy." At the time when Roosevelt requested help from Sweden for the large remaining group of Jews in Budapest, the decision as to who would be sent to Hungary was delegated primarily to Iver Olsen, a representative of the War Refugee Board but, unknown to many, also part of the OSS (Office of Strategic Services), later to become the CIA. Basing their view on that connection, along with their interpretation of other now declassified papers, some feel that Raoul Wallenberg went to Budapest as a spy for the United States. It is not the purpose of this book to deal with this issue in depth. However, because the question has now been raised in such a public way, it does need to be addressed.

In the first place, according to Anger and further documented by an Associated Press release, when Iver Olsen was questioned in 1955 by the CIA, he denied rumors that Wallenberg was a spy. Anger also stated to me that Wallenberg did not even know of Olsen's OSS connections. Wallenberg was not salaried by the OSS. Furthermore, the notion that he could send out espionage communications through the diplomatic pouch was impossible since Anger regularly inspected the contents of that pouch. In addition, Anger was in almost daily contact with Wallenberg, and he feels that not only was Wallenberg not a spy but that his twenty-four-hours-a-day rescue work would have precluded any such action.

Apart from the issue of whether or not Wallenberg was a spy, it also seems highly illogical that the Soviets could ever justify the imprisonment of Wallenberg for being a spy against the Nazis, since such espionage activity would, after all, place Wallenberg on the side of the Russians, not against them.

What seems tragic about this recent media outburst is that it tends to whitewash the Soviets in their criminal action against Wallenberg as well as detract from the truly humanitarian, self-sacrificing motives of Wallenberg's wartime activities. Perhaps we have a world today that is becoming so depleted of real heroes that we have some need to deny their existence when they do come to light.

Congressman Tom Lantos said it well in his comment relating to the decision of the U.S. Postal Service to issue a postal stamp to pay tribute to Wallenberg. Said Lantos: "In an age with few heroes, it is most appropriate that we celebrate that true heroism of Raoul Wallenberg with a United States stamp in his honor."[31]

Per Anger, another hero from those days in Budapest, was honored by Sweden for his work in Hungary with the Royal Order of Vasa as well as with similar decorations from Holland, Finland, and Persia (now Iran) for the part he took in safeguarding these countries' interests in Hungary during the war years.

In 1987 Hungary showed its gratitude for the Swedish rescue work by erecting an impressive Wallenberg monument in Budapest and later by installing a plaque on the old legation building with the profiles and names of Danielsson, Wallenberg, and Anger.

In November 1995, Anger was presented with a medal at a B'nai B'rith conference in Budapest. At the same time, at a ceremony in the parliament, the Hungarian president awarded Anger a distinguished decoration for his work on behalf of Wallenberg.

While researching this book, I received a touching letter from Max Grunberg of the Raoul Wallenberg Honorary Citizen Committee in Israel. Describing a time when

Anger was asked to visit Canada and speak, he gives this testimony:

> I witnessed, as Per was received with a standing ovation by the House of Commons.
>
> When we had to say good-bye to each other, Per said: "Max, please, never forget the story of Raoul." These words are since then engraved in my heart.
>
> But most important, Per would always talk about Raoul and not about his own involvement in this rescue operation. Only when pressed for an answer, Per would say in a very humble tone: "I helped Raoul" and would immediately go back to speaking about Raoul.
>
> Therefore in all honesty I have not had much of a chance to learn about "the real Per," as he would always talk to me as if "Raoul was talking to me about his deeds." And this is precisely the most important lesson we can learn about Per, namely he is always putting Raoul and the search for Raoul as his priority in life.[32]

Anyone who has heard Ambassador Anger speak could echo these words regarding his lifelong loyalty to Raoul Wallenberg. His desire to find him has run like a thread throughout his whole life since Budapest. It is the desire around which so much of his life has revolved, and as such, in many ways it defines Per Anger.

Per Anger, Consul General of Sweden, San Francisco, 1963, on his fiftieth birthday. *(Courtesy of Per Anger family.)*

Ambassador Per Anger with The Right Honourable Jules Léger after presenting his credentials to the Canadian government, Ottawa, Canada, in 1976. *(Courtesy of Per Anger family.)*

YAD VASHEM
HarHazikaron
Jérusalem

יד ושם
הר הזיכרון
ירושלים

DANS LE SOUVENIR
RÉSIDE LE SECRET
DE LA RÉDEMPTION
(Baal Chem Tov)

תעודה
ATTESTATION

שם נפשו בכפו להצלת יהודים בתקופת השואה.

AU PERIL DE SA VIE A SAUVE DES JUIFS PENDANT L'HOLOCAUSTE

נטע עץ בשדרת חסידי אומות העולם

A PLANTE UN ARBRE DANS L'ALLEE DES JUSTES

LE **9 Mai 1983** ביום כו אייר תשמ"ג

בשם רשות הזיכרון יד-ושם
Pour l'Institut du Souvenir Yad Vashem

בשם הוועדה לציון חסידי אומות העולם
Pour la Commission des Justes

...ונתתי להם בביתי ובחומותי יד ושם... אשר לא יכרת. ישעיהו נ"ו
...JE LEUR DONNERAI UNE PLACE ET UN NOM... QUI NE PERIRA PAS... ESAIE, 56

The certificate Per Anger received when he was honored by Israel as one who is "Righteous among the Nations," a title given to non-Jews who risked their lives to save Jews during the Holocaust. Those so recognized are also awarded a medal and have a tree planted in Jerusalem. *(Courtesy of Per Anger family.)*

Ambassador Per Anger presenting his book, *With Raoul Wallenberg in Budapest,* to the president of Israel, Chaim Herzog (president 1983–1993). *(Courtesy of Per Anger family.)*

Per Anger and his wife, Elena, welcomed to the Swedish Club in San Francisco, 1987. *(Courtesy of Per Anger family.)*

Per Anger in San Francisco in 1987 speaking at the Swedish Club with Swedish Consul General Siri Eliason and Congressman Tom Lantos and his wife, Annette. *(Courtesy of Per Anger family.)*

Inauguration of a plaque on the wall of the former Swedish Legation building honoring Carl-Ivan Danielsson, Raoul Wallenberg, and Per Anger. Budapest, July 9, 1994. *(Courtesy of Per Anger family.)*

161

The President of Hungary, Gönez Arpád, conferring an award on Ambassador Per Anger in Hungary, 1995. At the time the president expressed his regrets that it had taken fifty years for Hungary to bestow such an honor upon Anger. *(Photographer: Isza Ferenc.)*

Ambassador Per Anger in Bonn, Germany, with the President of Germany Roman Herzog in June 1995. From left to right: Max Grünberg of Israel, founder of the Raoul Wallenberg Committee in Israel; Orjian Berner, the Swedish Ambassador; President Herzog; and Ambassador Per Anger. *(Courtesy of Per Anger family.)*

162

Ambassador Per Anger and his wife, Elena, with Consul General Walter Danielson and his wife, Beryl (January 1995). *(Photographer: David Swerdlin. Used by permission.)*

Per Anger in his office in Stockholm in 1985. Wallenberg's picture is in the background. *(Courtesy of Per Anger family.)*

163

Per Anger speaking in Washington, D.C., at the United States Holocaust Memorial Museum, January 17, 1995, commemorating Raoul Wallenberg's arrest fifty years earlier by the then Soviet Union. *(Courtesy of Per Anger family.)*

Man with a Message

Two well-built fires in the fireplaces augmented the lights in the living room and adjoining sitting room. Over the sitting room hearth hung the blue and yellow Swedish coat of arms. Framed pictures of foreign dignitaries were placed on antique furniture. Finely executed, original paintings hung on the walls, and in general one had a sense of another time, another place, where small touches of elegance were important and good manners were automatically a way of life. The atmosphere was enchanting.

At the large dining room table, Ambassador Per Anger and his wife were seated in places of honor. Anger's hair was now snow-white. No longer the young secretary of the legation, he was now a retired ambassador, the father of three, and the grandfather of three, but he had lost none of his elegance or charm.

Outside the snow was not piled up in deep drifts, nor was the air cold. No air-raid warnings or gunshots sounded. Instead it was a spring day, a bit chilly only by Southern California standards. Instead of 1944 the year was 1989.

Soon the conversation of the past superseded the present, and one became absorbed in a world that was the world of the 1940s and World War II Europe. The name *Wallenberg* was brought up, with ongoing concern for his whereabouts.

Anger turned the conversation reflectively to Sweden and his boyhood days. He talked of returning to the mountains where he used to play as a young boy and of talking to God while he drew strength from his boyhood memories. He spoke of his safety zones, and I realized that long before he had used that term, he had always had places, things, people, and beliefs that sustained and refreshed him. His safety zones had helped him to survive, and, indeed, they had enabled him to help others over a long period of time.

Another factor that enabled Anger to persevere under all kinds of difficult conditions was his own background and personality. His fellow diplomat in Budapest, Lars Berg, described Anger from his observation of him during the difficult and dangerous war years as "not only a skillful and hardworking diplomat," but "also a loyal and cheerful friend, whose everlasting good humor was a valuable help to us all. Even in very serious times . . . he could, at a late dinner, shake off all the weariness and worries and get us all into a light and gay mood."[1]

Anger's capacity for refurbishment and cheerfulness was not just a pleasant escape from the realities of life. His ability to recharge his energies and to find inspiration helped him in situations most people could not handle. He saw suffering and fought for the helpless with a rare courage.

A man well prepared personally combined with a time of history that offered the opportunity, and the development of a hero resulted. Ambassador Per Anger has appropriately been honored by Israel as one who is "Righteous among the Nations," which is a title for non-Jews who risked their lives to save Jews during the Holocaust. The name comes from a Hebrew phrase, *hasidei ummot haolam,* used by the rabbis of the Talmud, who stated: "The righteous among the nations of the world have a place in the world to come." The Martyrs' and Heroes' Remembrance *(Yad Vashem)* Law, passed by Israel's Knesset (Parliament) in 1953, charged the Yad Vashem Remembrance Authority with perpetuating and establishing a memorial to "the Righteous among the Nations who risked their lives to save Jews."[2]

The term *Righteous among the Gentiles* or *Righteous Gentile* refers to all who extend kindness to Jews in time of trouble. "However, in the context of the Martyrs' and Heroes' Remembrance law, it is clear that loftier requirements were required to qualify as 'Righteous among the Nations who risked their lives to save Jews.'" When the committee decides who is eligible for this honor they use three main criteria:

1. A concrete rescue action or aid in rescue
2. Rescue carried out at personal risk
3. Remuneration neither requested nor received by the rescuer for the action or aid[3]

Those recognized as Righteous Gentiles are awarded a medal, a certificate, and a tree that is planted in a designated area in Israel. On the medal are engraved the words: "He who saves one life is considered as having saved the whole universe."[4]

As of July 1995 there were 13,223 Righteous Gentiles so honored. Among these are names like ten Boom, Schindler, Wallenberg, and Per Anger. In comparison with those who needed rescue, and who in some instances could have been rescued, the numbers are small. But they are bright lights in the darkness of the Holocaust, and they show that one person can indeed make a difference.

Many of the Gentiles so honored have been Christians. For the Christian the saving of the life of a Jew has a special meaning for, according to the teachings of both the Old and New Testaments, the Jews are God's chosen race, the race through which God promised to send Messiah and the race through whom, according to Christian teaching, Messiah did indeed come in the person of Jesus Christ. It was of Christ that John, known historically as John the Baptist, spoke. Since John may well have eaten of the carob tree in his sojourn in the wilderness, in a gracious gesture, the carob tree has been used to designate the Righteous Gentile.

The message of Per Anger's life is that in small ways as well as large, one person can make a difference. That difference may be saving the lives of hundreds of Jews, or it may be a small, simple difference.

As I was Christmas shopping last year, I almost automatically dropped some money in the Salvation Army pot, where money is collected for the poor. I was reminded that for some reason I can't even remember, a few years ago there was a movement to ban such collections. In her memoirs former First Lady Barbara Bush refers to that time and tells how in order to make a statement she made sure she went to the one mall that had not banned the donation pot.[5]

In 1995 the Salvation Army handed out small, attractive cards with the words: "You Make the Difference. God Bless You." On the back of the card is a small picture related to Christmas. The picture folds out and inside is a Bible verse and a devotional thought. Inside my card were the words: "I believe God's power is there, not because I feel it, but because it is a fact." The words "You Make the Difference" put the responsibility and the reward on me, even if the sacrifice was not great at all.

One of my patients made a difference in another way. She came in and declared that she and her husband had decided not to exchange gifts at Christmas. They gave gifts to their children, then with the rest of their Christmas money, supplemented by money that friends donated, they bought gifts and food for a family who had experienced very hard times. The wife had become ill, and at the same time the husband had lost his job. The couple and their four children could barely afford food. Celebrating Christmas was not even considered until my patient and her husband decided to give up part of their own Christmas and share it.

On Christmas Eve of that same year, a piece was printed in a Los Angeles newspaper that excerpted a long quote from Charles Colson's book, *The Body*. It told of a "Righteous Gentile," Maximilian Kolbe. Before Poland was invaded by the Nazis, this Polish friar said to his fellow friars: "An atrocious conflict is brewing. We do not know what will develop. In our beloved Poland, we must expect the worst."[6] In the fall of 1939 Poland was invaded by Germany.

Kolbe was eventually taken to Auschwitz because, as a priest, he would not follow Nazi orders. One day someone escaped from the camp, and as was so frequently the case, the Nazis selected ten prisoners who would die because of the one man who escaped. One man so chosen cried out: "My poor wife! My poor children! What will they do?"[7]

Suddenly Kolbe broke out from the line—something a prisoner never dared to do. To do so and to address a Nazi officer were excuse for execution. The soft voice was calm as he said to the Nazi butcher: "I would like to die in place of one of the men you condemned."

"Why?" barked the commandant.

"I am an old man, sir, and good for nothing. My life will serve no purpose."

169

The ploy worked, for in his next breath the commandant asked: "In whose place do you want to die?"

"For that one," Kolbe responded, pointing to the weeping prisoner who had bemoaned his wife and children.

For the first and last time, the commandant looked Kolbe in the eye. "Who are you?" he said.

The prisoner looked back at him, a strange fire in his dark eyes. "I am a priest."

"Ein Pfaffe!" he snorted. Then number 5659 was replaced on the death list by number 16670.[8] Number 16670 had made a difference. Number 16670 was by all definitions a "Righteous Gentile."

Regardless of the magnitude of the task, each of us does in one way or another make a difference for good or evil in the lives of those around us. We each choose the difference we make.

Though Per Anger eventually left Budapest, with its daily life and death struggles, his message did not change, for in many ways Budapest had changed the course of his life forever. Ten years after Hugo Wohl stood at his door in Budapest's dark night, Anger once again had the opportunity to help Wohl's family. By this time Wohl's daughter Edit and her husband Lars were living in Sweden, but Hugo Wohl was still in Budapest. Sitting by the telephone in Sweden, Lars Ernster wondered if there were not some more effective way to ensure the safety of his wife's parents. Certainly going to Vienna was a start. As Dr. Ernster said to me:

One hundred and forty thousand Hungarians were leaving the country . . . and I went out every night to the border, which is only twenty miles from Vienna, to try to help people to get over and to get some help. But there was also a very strong Swedish delegation that the Red Cross sent. . . . One day I went to the Swedish embassy in Vienna to ask Anger, because I knew he was there. . . . I went to him because . . . I knew he knew me. And I knew that he knew her father. And so I said: "Give me personal advice. Shall I dare to try to get on one of those Red Cross cars that went . . . right over the border to help refugees?"

Should he go and try to find his wife's family?

Anger's advice may well have saved Lars Ernster's life for the second time. "May I give you personal advice?" he asked. Then, without waiting for an answer, he exhorted Ernster: "Don't do it! Don't do it! Don't do it!" Anger explained that in spite of using Red Cross cars, one could never be sure of what the Russians might do. The Ernsters were Swedish citizens, but because they were born in Hungary, that citizenship might not count in the minds of the Russians. In Anger's opinion, the risk was not worth the result, because it was very possible that the Wohls might more easily just emigrate over the border. And that is exactly what happened. The result was that the Wohl family was saved without added risk.[9] Once again the life of Per Anger had made a difference.

Dr. Lars Ernster was a firsthand witness from the war years and the uprising. Years later Anger told me: "I remember when they gave me the medal in the Israeli Embassy in Stockholm and they planted my tree later on. Sitting in the first row in the ceremony at the embassy was Ernster, and I could well understand that. They had been behind all this."[10]

In terms of career status, the pinnacle of Anger's success was when he was named ambassador. Perhaps he was better prepared for such an honor than most. When he was just entering the foreign service as an attaché, he had been given wise advice by an older colleague. The older man admonished:

Remember, your ambassador one day will go on holiday. You will be in charge of the embassy. You will be chargé d'affaires. Then all of a sudden you will meet heads of state. You will be called upon to be at big ceremonies and receptions, and people will be very polite to you, and they will call you "Your Excellency" and all that. If you don't understand immediately then that it's not you who's a very famous person, that it's not *your* personality, if you go around thinking, "I didn't know that I was that prominent a person," then you might as well leave the foreign service immediately.

You have to understand that you are there in an official capacity. It's not you, it's the role, it's the representation. It's that you represent your country that counts, and forget about yourself.[11]

Speaking of his own evolving personal philosophy, Anger once said pensively: "Very often I think of this wonderful life I have had and how privileged I've been. And then I've thought of how life is kind of a theater, a spectacle . . . and you are not yourself. You are influenced by your friends, by other people, by your profession. Especially in my profession you have to keep your feelings. You can't say whatever you think."

Reflecting on the tremendous pressure of being in the spotlight and of moving in international circles, Anger continued: "You are born as a child, as a baby. You are born as an original person. . . . Then, after you grow up, you are formed by the environment to something which is not the real you. So that is my wish, that I could go back and be a child again in the sense that one could be more natural and not mind what other people think."[12]

More fundamental to his basic beliefs, however, are old-fashioned virtues like honesty, loyalty, and friendship. While he believes that everyone should do the best job possible, he also believes that "every profession is a good profession, and there is no profession which is lower or not as important as any other."

172

In talking about his first job with the foreign service, when he was sent to Berlin, Anger reminisced that he was not really trained in economics, even though his job required him to deal with economic questions. Claimed Anger: "I was sitting up whole nights trying to write reports. . . . And I said to myself . . . I can't do more than my best. Then I felt I could help if I had that in mind." At times like that he always felt, "You get help from God." That attitude and these values have continued throughout his life.

Anger has made a difference in many lives. For some he was an encouragement, a help in saving a business, a way of locating a relative. For others, he literally saved their lives. His legacy of action will live on long after his own life ends.

In a speech following a dinner at the Swedish consul general's home in Los Angeles, California, Per Anger concluded his words on Raoul Wallenberg with: "Wallenberg has become a symbol for all of our fight for human rights. Wallenberg was one of the greatest humanitarians of our time."

Some questions were asked, then a few comments followed, one by a Hungarian who had helped Wallenberg. The atmosphere was charged with the emotion of the events of fifty years ago.

Then in the moment of silence that would have preceded the end, an elderly, stately Jewish man rose to his feet.

"Mr. Ambassador," he began in a slow but forceful tone of voice. "This is not a question. This is a statement that comes from the bottom of my heart. There is a Jewish saying that the world is supported at any given time by thirty-six righteous men. Nobody knows who they are. But I think that Raoul Wallenberg, the one we are talking about today, is one of them. And you, Mr. Ambassador, are one of the others. Thank you very much."

The group was silent. There was nothing else to ask or to say, for no one could have summed up the life of this great man more appropriately.

At the commemoration of Raoul Wallenberg at the United States Holocaust Memorial Museum, Washington, D.C., on the occasion of the fiftieth anniversary of his disappearance, Hungarian ambassador Dr. György Bánlaki remarked:

We ought

To recall: how easy it still is to infatuate people
             how defenseless society is against lies
                 frequently repeated
             how daring you should be to stand up
             against false, but publicly accepted
             prophets

To realize: how quickly
             intolerance slips into prejudice
             prejudice into discrimination
             discrimination into stigmatization
             stigmatization into condemnation
             condemnation into hatred

To remember:
             how grateful we should be for having among
                 us people
             who are clear of mind
                 open of heart
                 brave of soul
                 strong of will
                 compassionate and merciful

Raoul Wallenberg was such a man.[13]

Per Anger, too, is such a man, along with all those who are willing to pay the price to make a difference. That *is* the message of Per Anger.

Notes

Preface

1. *Per* is pronounced to rhyme with "pear," and *Anger* rhymes with "hunger."

2. Per Anger, *With Raoul Wallenberg in Budapest: Memories of the War Years in Hungary,* trans. David Mel Paul and Margareta Paul (New York: Holocaust Library, 1981). Reprinted (Washington, D.C.: Holocaust Library, an imprint of the United States Holocaust Memorial Museum, 1996).

Chapter 1: One Man Can Make a Difference

1. Personal interview with Ambassador Per Anger.

2. Ibid.

3. Max Hastings, *Victory in Europe: D-Day to V-E Day* (Boston: Little, Brown & Co., 1985), 54.

4. Raoul Wallenberg, *Letters and Dispatches 1924–1944,* trans. Kjersti Board (New York: Arcade, 1995), 216–17.

5. Lars G. Berg, *The Book That Disappeared: What Happened in Budapest* (New York: Vantage Press, 1990), 6.

6. Raul Hilberg, *The Destruction of the European Jews* (Chicago: Quadrangle Books, 1961), 533–34.

7. Berg, *The Book That Disappeared,* 54–55.

8. Hilberg, *Destruction of the European Jews,* 666.

9. Corrie ten Boom with John and Elizabeth Sherrill, *The Hiding Place* (Minneapolis: Worldwide, 1971), 113.

Chapter 2: Preparation for Conflict

1. Personal interview with Ambassador Per Anger.

2. Berg, *The Book That Disappeared,* 62–75, paraphrased.

3. Personal interview with Ambassador Per Anger.

4. Personal papers from Ambassador Per Anger.

5. Ibid.

6. Berg, *The Book That Disappeared,* 10, 53, paraphrased.

7. Elizabeth R. Skoglund, *Safety Zones* (Grand Rapids: Baker, 1986).

8. Personal interview with Ambassador Per Anger.

Chapter 3: Inside the Swedish Legation

1. Letter from Iver Olsen (Stockholm) to U.S. State Department, 14 August 1944.

2. Ibid., paraphrased.

3. Personal interview with Ambassador Per Anger.

4. Ibid.

5. Anger, *With Raoul Wallenberg in Budapest,* 32–33.

6. Berg, *The Book That Disappeared,* 6–7, paraphrased.

7. Sharon Linnéa, *Raoul Wallenberg, the Man Who Stopped Death* (Philadelphia: The Jewish Publication Society, 1993), 95, paraphrased.

8. Kati Marton, *Wallenberg* (New York: Random House, 1982), 119.

9. Personal interview with Thomas Veres.

10. Personal interview with Dr. and Mrs. Lars Ernster.

11. Personal interview with Kate Wacz.

12. Personal interview with Ambassador Per Anger.

13. Ibid.

14. Berg, *The Book That Disappeared,* 9–12, paraphrased.

15. Ibid., 12.

16. Ibid., 53.

17. Jeno (Eugene) Levai, *Black Book on the Martyrdom of Hungarian Jewry,* vol.

1 (Zurich, Switzerland: Central European Times, 1948), 77.

18. Personal interview with Ambassador Per Anger.

19. Ibid.

Chapter 4: Rescuer

1. Simon Wiesenthal Library and Archives, Los Angeles, Calif.

2. Ibid.

3. Ibid.

4. Marton, *Wallenberg,* 109–10.

5. Ibid., 112–13.

6. Ibid., 140. Note that estimates of the numbers of Jews in the ghetto constantly fluctuated because the number who were there varied from day to day.

7. Alan Levy, *The Wiesenthal File* (Grand Rapids: Eerdmans, 1993), 194.

8. Jeno (Eugene) Levai, *Raoul Wallenberg: His Remarkable Life, Heroic Battles, and the Secret of His Mysterious Disappearance,* trans. Frank Vajda (Melbourne, Australia: University of Melbourne, 1989), 214.

9. Ibid., 15.

10. Ibid., 21.

11. Wallenberg, *Letters and Dispatches,* 186–87.

12. Ibid., 173.

13. Personal interview with Ambassador Per Anger.

14. Ibid.

15. Simon Wiesenthal Library and Archives, Los Angeles, Calif.

16. Personal interview with Ambassador Per Anger.

17. Ibid.

18. Wallenberg, *Letters and Dispatches,* 92.

19. Levai, *Raoul Wallenberg,* 23.

20. Ibid., 28.

21. Anger, *With Raoul Wallenberg in Budapest,* 86.

22. Levai, *Raoul Wallenberg,* 215–16, paraphrased.

23. Ibid., 236.

Chapter 5: One Man's Imprint for Evil

1. Simon Wiesenthal Library and Archives, Los Angeles, Calif.

2. C. H. Spurgeon, *The Metropolitan Tabernacle Pulpit, Sermons Preached and Revised,* vol. 9 (Pasadena, Tex.: Pilgrim Publications, 1970), 399–400.

3. Hannah Arendt, *Eichmann in Jerusalem: A Report on the Banality of Evil* (New York: Penguin Books, 1963), 27.

4. Ibid.

5. John Donovan, *Eichmann Man of Slaughter* (New York: Avon, 1960), 98.

6. Arendt, *Eichmann in Jerusalem,* 252.

7. Paul West, *The Very Rich Hours of Count von Stauffenberg* (New York: Harper & Row, 1980), 152.

8. Ibid., 153.

9. Randolph L. Braham, *The Politics of Genocide: The Holocaust in Hungary,* vol. 1 (New York: Columbia University Press, 1981), 396.

10. Personal interview with Ambassador Per Anger.

11. Levy, *Wiesenthal File,* 153.

12. Arendt, *Eichmann in Jerusalem,* 140.

13. Jochen von Lang, ed., in collaboration with Claus Sibyll, *Eichmann Interrogated: Transcripts from the Archives of the Israeli Police,* trans. Ralph Manheim (New York: Farrar, Straus, & Giroux, 1983), 203.

14. Wallenberg, *Letters and Dispatches,* 217.

15. Arendt, *Eichmann in Jerusalem,* 25.

16. Personal interview with Ambassador Per Anger.

17. *The Trial of Adolf Eichmann,* Record of Proceedings in the District Court of Jerusalem, vol. 4 (Jerusalem: State of Israel Ministry of Justice, 1992), 1533.

18. Levy, *Wiesenthal File,* 89.

19. Ibid., 111.

20. Arendt, *Eichmann in Jerusalem,* 273.

21. Braham, *Politics of Genocide,* vol. 1, 395.

22. Richard Jerome, Terry Smith, Dietlind Lerner, Abe Rabinovich, "Sins

of the Fathers," *People Magazine* (10 July 1995), 44–45.

23. Berg, *The Book That Disappeared,* 14–15, paraphrased.

24. Ibid., 15.

25. Personal interview with Ambassador Per Anger.

Chapter 6: Battlefield of Wits

1. Personal interview with Kate Wacz.

2. Braham, *Politics of Genocide,* vol. 1, 79–80.

3. Personal interview with Ambassador Per Anger.

4. From a speech given by Dr. Frank Vajda, chairman of the Free Wallenberg Australian Committee, on the occasion of Ambassador Per Anger's seventy-fifth birthday celebration. Stockholm, 7 December 1988.

5. Anger, *With Raoul Wallenberg in Budapest,* 43.

6. Simon Wiesenthal Library and Archives, Los Angeles, Calif.

7. Ibid.

8. Personal interview with Kate Wacz.

9. Levai, *Raoul Wallenberg,* 89.

10. Mary Williams Walsh, "Swiss Finally Clear Rescuer of World War II Jews," *Los Angeles Times* (1 December 1995).

11. Elizabeth R. Skoglund, *Life on the Line* (Wheaton, Ill.: Tyndale House, 1989), 102–3.

12. Personal interview with Ambassador Per Anger.

13. Wallenberg, *Letters and Dispatches,* 218.

14. Personal interview with Ambassador Per Anger.

15. Simon Wiesenthal Library and Archives, Los Angeles, Calif.

16. Personal interview with Ambassador Per Anger.

17. Agnes Adachi, *Child of the Winds: My Mission with Raoul Wallenberg* (Chicago: Adams Press, 1989), 10.

18. Levai, *Martyrdom of Hungarian Jewry,* 402, 447.

19. Braham, *Politics of Genocide,* vol. 2, 837.

20. David S. Wyman, *The Abandonment of the Jews: America and the Holocaust, 1941–1945* (New York: Pantheon Books, 1984), 241.

21. Personal interview with Ambassador Per Anger.

22. Braham, *Politics of Genocide,* vol. 2, 841–42.

23. Levai, *Raoul Wallenberg,* 135.

24. Personal interview with Ambassador Per Anger.

25. Ibid.

26. From a speech given by Hugh J. Schwartzberg, secretary of the Raoul Wallenberg Committee of Chicago, on the occasion of Ambassador Per Anger's address to the committee, 13 October 1987.

Chapter 7: Mr. Ambassador

1. *Sunday Morning,* CBS News, 23 April 1995.

2. Personal papers from Ambassador Per Anger.

3. Anger, *With Raoul Wallenberg in Budapest,* 145.

4. Personal interview with Ambassador Per Anger.

5. Ibid.

6. Anger, *With Raoul Wallenberg in Budapest,* 154.

7. Personal interview with Ambassador Per Anger.

8. Personal papers from Ambassador Per Anger.

9. Sir Winston Churchill, *The Second World War,* vol. 6 (Boston: Houghton Mifflin, 1953), 772.

10. George Mikes, *The Hungarian Revolution* (London: Andre Deutsch, 1957), 27–28.

11. The editors of Time-Life Books, *WW II: Time-Life Books History of the Second World War* (New York: Time-Life Books, 1989), 460.

12. Ibid.

13. Mikes, *Hungarian Revolution,* 31.

14. Adachi, *Child of the Winds,* 21.

15. Mikes, *Hungarian Revolution,* 128.

16. Martin Caidin, *The Tigers Are Burning* (New York: Hawthorn Books, 1974), 124.

17. Ibid., 124–25, paraphrased.

18. Berg, *The Book That Disappeared*, 195.

19. Anger, *With Raoul Wallenberg in Budapest*, 128.

20. Mikes, *Hungarian Revolution*, 174–75.

21. Personal interview with Ambassador Per Anger.

22. Personal papers from Ambassador Per Anger.

23. Ibid.

24. Personal interview and papers from Ambassador Per Anger.

25. Personal papers from Ambassador Per Anger.

26. Ibid.

27. Personal interview and papers from Ambassador Per Anger.

28. Personal papers from Ambassador Per Anger.

29. Ibid.

30. Ibid.

31. Congressman Tom Lantos, press release, 6 May 1996.

32. Personal letter from Max Grunberg, 28 February 1995.

Chapter 8: Man with a Message

1. Berg, *The Book That Disappeared*, 53.

2. Moshe Bejski, "Righteous Among the Nations," ed. Israel Gutman, *Encyclopedia of the Holocaust*, vol. 3 (New York: Macmillan, 1990), 1279.

3. Ibid., 1281.

4. Ibid.

5. Barbara Bush, *Barbara Bush: A Memoir* (New York: St. Martin's Paperbacks, 1994), 336.

6. Charles Colson, "Faith Conquers Hate," *Daily News*, 24 December 1995.

7. Ibid.

8. Ibid.

9. Personal interview with Dr. and Mrs. Lars Ernster.

10. Personal interview with Ambassador Per Anger.

11. Ibid.

12. Ibid.

13. Remarks by Hungarian Ambassador Dr. György Bánlaki, at the commemoration of Raoul Wallenberg on the occasion of the 50th anniversary of his disappearance, United States Holocaust Memorial Museum, Washington, D.C., 17 January 1995.

Bibliography

Adachi, Agnes. *Child of the Winds: My Mission with Raoul Wallenberg.* Chicago: Adams Press, 1989.

Anger, Per. *With Raoul Wallenberg in Budapest: Memories of the War Years in Hungary.* Trans. David Mel Paul and Margareta Paul. New York: Holocaust Library, 1981. Reprinted 1996 by the Holocaust Library, an imprint of the United States Holocaust Memorial Museum, Washington, D.C.

Arendt, Hannah. *Eichmann in Jerusalem: A Report on the Banality of Evil.* New York: Penguin Books, 1963.

Astor, Gerald. *The "Last" Nazi: The Life and Times of Dr. Joseph Mengele.* New York: Fine, 1985.

Baedeker, Karl. *Austria Together with Budapest, Prague, Karlsbad, and Marienbad, Handbook for Travellers.* New York: Scribners, 1929.

Berg, Lars G. *The Book That Disappeared: What Happened in Budapest.* New York: Vantage Press, 1990.

Bierman, John. *Righteous Gentile: The Story of Raoul Wallenberg, Missing Hero of the Holocaust.* New York: Viking, 1981.

Blau, Leslie. *Bonyhad, a Destroyed Community: The Jews of Bonyhad, Hungary.* New York: Shengold, 1994.

Bonhoeffer, Dietrich. *Letters and Papers from Prison.* New York: Macmillan, 1971.

Braham, Randolph L. *The Politics of Genocide: The Holocaust in Hungary.* 2 vols. New York: Columbia University, 1981.

———, ed. *The Tragedy of Hungarian Jewry.* New York: Columbia University, 1986.

Brown, Anthony Cave. *Bodyguard of Lies.* New York: Bantam, 1975.

Caidin, Martin. *The Tigers Are Burning.* New York: Hawthorn Books, 1974.

Churchill, Winston S. *The Second World War.* 6 vols. Boston: Houghton Mifflin, 1953.

Cohen, Asher. *The Halutz Resistance in Hungary 1942–1944.* New York: Columbia University, 1986.

Donovan, John. *Eichmann Man of Slaughter.* New York: Avon, 1960.

Dumbach, Annette, and Jud Newborn. *Shattering the German Night: The Story of the White Rose.* Boston: Little, Brown & Co., 1986.

The Editors of Time-Life Books. *WW II: Time-Life Books History of the Second World War.* New York: Time-Life Books, 1989.

Eman, Diet, with James Schaap. *Things We Couldn't Say.* Grand Rapids: Eerdmans, 1994.

Evans, Richard J. *In Hitler's Shadow.* New York: Pantheon, 1989.

Frankl, Viktor E. *The Doctor and the Soul.* New York: Vintage, 1973.

———. *Man's Search for Meaning.* New York: Pocket Books, 1985.

Gies, Miep, with Allison Leslie Gold. *Anne Frank Remembered: The Story of the Woman Who Helped to Hide the Frank Family.* New York: Simon & Schuster, 1987.

Gill, Anton. *The Journey Back from Hell, an Oral History: Conversations with Concentration Camp Survivors.* New York: William Morrow, 1988.

Gutman, Israel, ed. *Encyclopedia of the Holocaust.* Vol. 3. New York: Macmillan, 1990.

Bibliography

Hallie, Phillip. *Lest Innocent Blood Be Shed*. New York: Harper & Row, 1979.

Harel, Isser. *The House on Garibaldi Street: The First Full Account of the Capture of Adolf Eichmann Told by the Former Head of Israel's Secret Service*. New York: Viking, 1975.

Hastings, Max. *Victory in Europe: D-Day to V-E Day*. Boston: Little, Brown & Co., 1985.

Hersh, Gizelle, and Peggy Mann. *"Gizelle, Save the Children!"* New York: Everest, 1980.

Hilberg, Raul. *Destruction of the European Jews*. Chicago: Quadrangle Books, 1961.

Hitler, Adolf. *Mein Kampf*. New York: Stackpole Sons, 1939.

International Committee of the Red Cross and the Jews in Hungary, The, 1943–1945. *Facing the Holocaust in Budapest*. Boston: Kluwer, 1988.

Katzburg, Nathaniel. *Hungary and the Jews: Policy and Legislation 1928–1943*. Israel: Bar-Ilan University, 1981.

Keneally, Thomas. *Schindler's List*. New York: Simon & Schuster, 1982.

Lang, Jochen von, ed., in collaboration with Claus Sibyll. *Eichmann Interrogated: Transcripts from the Archives of the Israeli Police*. Trans. Ralph Manheim. New York: Farrar, Straus & Giroux, 1983.

Laqueur, Walter. *The Terrible Secret: Suppression of the Truth about Hitler's "Final Solution."* Boston: Little, Brown & Co., 1980.

Lester, Elenore. *Wallenberg the Man in the Iron Web*. Englewood Cliffs, N.J.: Prentice-Hall, 1982.

Levai, Jeno (Eugene). *Black Book on the Martyrdom of Hungarian Jewry*. Zurich, Switzerland: Central European Times, 1948.

———. *Eichmann in Hungary*. Budapest, Hungary: Pannonia, 1961.

———. *Raoul Wallenberg: His Remarkable Life, Heroic Battles, and the Secret of His Mysterious Disappearance*. Trans. Frank Vajda. Melbourne, Australia: University of Melbourne, 1989.

Levi, Primo. *If This Is a Man: Remembering Auschwitz*. New York: Summit Books, 1986.

Levy, Alan. *The Wiesenthal File*. Grand Rapids: Eerdmans, 1993.

Lifton, Robert Jay. *The Nazi Doctors: Medical Killing and the Psychology of Genocide*. New York: Harper & Row, 1986.

Linnéa, Sharon. *Raoul Wallenberg, the Man Who Stopped Death*. Philadelphia: The Jewish Publications Society, 1993.

MacDonald, Callum. *The Killing of SS Obergruppenfuhrer Reinhard Heydrich*. New York: Macmillan, 1989.

Marton, Kati. *Wallenberg*. New York: Random House, 1982.

McCagg, William O., Jr. *Jewish Nobles and Geniuses in Modern Hungary*. New York: Columbia University, 1972.

Meltzer, Milton. *Rescue: The Story of How Gentiles Saved Jews in the Holocaust*. New York: Harper & Row, 1988.

Mikes, George. *The Hungarian Revolution*. London: Andre Deutsch, 1957.

Rolfe, William J., and William D. Crockett. *A Satchel Guide to Europe*. Rev. ed. Boston: Houghton Mifflin, 1929.

Shirer, William L. *The Challenge of Scandinavia, Norway, Sweden, Denmark, and Finland in Our Time*. London: Robert Hale, 1956.

———. *The Nightmare Years 1930–1940*. Vol. 2 of *Twentieth Century Journey*. Boston: Little, Brown & Co., 1984.

———. *The Rise and Fall of the Third Reich*. New York: Simon & Schuster, 1960.

Siegal, Aranka. *Upon the Head of the Goat: A Childhood in Hungary 1939–1944*. New York: New American Library, 1981.

Skoglund, Elizabeth R. *Life on the Line*. Wheaton, Ill.: Tyndale House, 1992.

———. *Safety Zones*. Grand Rapids: Baker, 1986.

ten Boom, Corrie, with John and Elizabeth Sherrill. *The Hiding Place*. Minneapolis: Worldwide, 1971.

The Trial of Adolf Eichmann. Record of Proceeding in the District Court of Jerusalem. 5 vols. Jerusalem: State of Israel Ministry of Justice, 1992.

Tusa, Ann, and John Tusa. *The Nuremberg Trial*. New York: Atheneum, 1983.

Wallenberg, Raoul. *Letters and Dispatches 1924–1944*. Trans. Kjersti Board. New York: Arcade, 1995.

Werbell, Frederick E., and Thurston Clarke. *Lost Hero: The Mystery of Raoul Wallenberg*. New York: McGraw-Hill, 1982.

West, Paul. *The Very Rich Hours of Count von Stauffenberg*. New York: Harper & Row, 1980.

Wiesel, Elie. *Night*. New York: Bantam, 1960.

Wiesenthal, Simon. *The Murderers Among Us: The Simon Wiesenthal Memoirs*. New York: McGraw-Hill, 1967.

———. *The Sunflower*. New York: Schocken, 1969.

Wood, E. Thomas, and Stanislaw M. Jankowski. *How One Man Tried to Stop the Holocaust*. New York: Wiley, 1994.

Wyman, David S. *The Abandonment of the Jews: America and the Holocaust, 1941–1945*. New York: Pantheon Books, 1984.

Acknowledgments

Previous to the writing of *A Quiet Courage,* any research that I have done on the Holocaust has been a dark encounter with evil. It was with some relief, therefore, that as I began to collect my data and write this book I realized that in writing about a man like Ambassador Per Anger there are bright lights even in the greatest times of human darkness. For his trust, his attention to detail, and for the wonderful story of his life, as well as for his patience and that of his family, I am grateful.

As always, but even more so in this book, I am indebted to my agent and friend Richard Baltzell for his hours of work, his encouragement, and his personal efforts for me in Budapest. In the same way, Rayne and Lance Wilcox have loyally typed, interviewed, attended to endless details, discovered old books, and in general supported the writing of this book in every way possible. My granddaughter, Elizabeth Hannah, in her own baby way, has provided a happy diversion as well as a constant reminder of the importance of each human life. Often when I have looked at her, I have thought of Jewish babies killed in the Holocaust. Her generation, too, must be taught about the Holocaust so that they and their children will never forget.

Without the consistent help of the Simon Wiesenthal Library and Archives in Los Angeles, the book would have been difficult to research. I am particularly indebted to Adaire Klein, Director of Library and Archival Services. Her patience, interest, breadth of knowledge as well as friendship have meant much. Aaron Breitbart, Senior Researcher, and Paul Hamburg, Reference Librarian, have always been generous with their time and vast reservoirs of knowledge. Amélie Dembitzer Levin, Library Assistant, and Fama Mor, Archivist, have also helped with research and photos. Rabbi Yitzchok Adlerstein, Director of Jewish Studies at Yeshiva University in Los Angeles, has once again willingly contributed from his profound grasp of the Hebrew language as well as his knowledge of Jewish history.

Benton Arnovitz, Director/Academic Publications, Genya Markon, Director of Photo Archives, and cartographer Dewey G. Hicks of the United States Holocaust Memorial Museum in Washington, D.C., as well as graphic artist Thach Nguyen, have provided direction as well as practical help in obtaining photographs, maps, and documents. For that I am in their debt.

Kate Kadelburger Wacz and Dr. Lars Ernster and his wife, Edit (Hugo Wohl's daughter), all survivors of those dark Budapest days, have given valuable assistance by their interviews as well as their unstinting help in obtaining photographs. Thomas Veres, a survivor as well as Wallenberg's personal photographer, was willing to share some of his legacy of Budapest through both interviews and photographs. Congressman and Mrs. Thomas Lantos gave generously of their support and time, as did the Congressman's Chief of Staff, Dr. Robert R. King. I am grateful also to another survivor, Agnes Adachi, for her verbal account, as well as to Gisela Weisz.

Within the Swedish community I am particularly indebted to Consul General Emeritus Walter Danielson and his wife, Beryl, and Honorary Consul General Siri M. Eliason. The Danielsons have opened up their home for interviews with the Ambassador as well as others, answered questions, informed me of coming events, and in general encouraged and supported me throughout the project. Siri Eliason has given time in interviews, translated the Ambassador's personal papers into English, provided historical data, and given much positive support. As a Swedish American the support of the Swedish community has held special significance.

I am grateful to Baker Books for publishing this book and specifically to Kin Millen, Dan Van't Kerkhoff, Mary Wenger, Allan Fisher, Twila Bennett, Joe Tremblay, and Dwight Baker. Pam McQuade's expertise as editor was also of great value.

So many others, too, have been helpful in such individual and unique ways. I am indebted to Max Grunberg and his deeply encouraging letter; Dr. Frank Vajda for sending a copy of his English translation of the hard-to-find Levai book on Wallenberg; and Stan Kurman of Needham Books.

I also wish to thank Jeffrey Schrier, Christian and Annmarie Early, Ruth Bell Graham, Evelyn and Don Freeland, Esther Copeland, Claudette Reiser, Marcia Means, Dianne Nevel, Pamela Reeve, Dr. and Mrs. John West, Dr. and Mrs. Kenneth Connolly, Dr. and Mrs. Matthew Conolly, Bruce and Martha Kober, Richard and Sandra Viola, Dave and Ruth Hunt, Charles Chefalo, Alan M. Homes, David M. Swerdlin, Martin Rosenfeld, Karl Weiskopf, Jozsef Nagy, and Cherie Rhodes.

To all of the above I express my deep thanks for support for a book that has been both difficult and deeply satisfying to write. To others too numerous to list I extend my gratitude also. A book like this has many threads and at the end it is difficult to trace all of their origins.

The people named above have been helpful in the writing of this book, but I alone am responsible for its content and viewpoint.

Index

Index

Index

Elizabeth Skoglund and Ambassador
Per Anger in 1995 in Los Angeles. *(Photographer: David Swerdlin. Used by
permission.)*

Elizabeth Ruth Skoglund has had a distinguished career as a teacher, counselor, and writer. She is the author of numerous books ranging in subject matter from psychological self-help, devotional, hospitality, bioethics, and children's stories to biographies of great people. Among these are *Loneliness, Safety Zones, Making Bad Times Good, Life on the Line, Wounded Heroes, and Amma*. For the last twenty-five years she has had a full-time counseling practice. Her time is divided between La Canada and Burbank, California. She became inspired to write *A Quiet Courage* after meeting Ambassador Per Anger for the first time at the Simon Wiesenthal Center, in Los Angeles, where he was speaking about Raoul Wallenberg.